BOKO HARAM: THE ISLAMIST INSURGENCY IN WEST AFRICA

HEARING

BEFORE THE

SUBCOMMITTEE ON TERRORISM, NONPROLIFERATION, AND TRADE

OF THE

COMMITTEE ON FOREIGN AFFAIRS HOUSE OF REPRESENTATIVES

ONE HUNDRED FOURTEENTH CONGRESS

SECOND SESSION

FEBRUARY 24, 2016

Serial No. 114–140

Printed for the use of the Committee on Foreign Affairs

Available via the World Wide Web: http://www.foreignaffairs.house.gov/ or http://www.gpo.gov/fdsys/

U.S. GOVERNMENT PUBLISHING OFFICE

98–829PDF   WASHINGTON : 2016

For sale by the Superintendent of Documents, U.S. Government Publishing Office
Internet: bookstore.gpo.gov   Phone: toll free (866) 512–1800; DC area (202) 512–1800
Fax: (202) 512–2104   Mail: Stop IDCC, Washington, DC 20402–0001

COMMITTEE ON FOREIGN AFFAIRS

EDWARD R. ROYCE, California, *Chairman*

CHRISTOPHER H. SMITH, New Jersey
ILEANA ROS-LEHTINEN, Florida
DANA ROHRABACHER, California
STEVE CHABOT, Ohio
JOE WILSON, South Carolina
MICHAEL T. McCAUL, Texas
TED POE, Texas
MATT SALMON, Arizona
DARRELL E. ISSA, California
TOM MARINO, Pennsylvania
JEFF DUNCAN, South Carolina
MO BROOKS, Alabama
PAUL COOK, California
RANDY K. WEBER SR., Texas
SCOTT PERRY, Pennsylvania
RON DeSANTIS, Florida
MARK MEADOWS, North Carolina
TED S. YOHO, Florida
CURT CLAWSON, Florida
SCOTT DesJARLAIS, Tennessee
REID J. RIBBLE, Wisconsin
DAVID A. TROTT, Michigan
LEE M. ZELDIN, New York
DANIEL DONOVAN, New York

ELIOT L. ENGEL, New York
BRAD SHERMAN, California
GREGORY W. MEEKS, New York
ALBIO SIRES, New Jersey
GERALD E. CONNOLLY, Virginia
THEODORE E. DEUTCH, Florida
BRIAN HIGGINS, New York
KAREN BASS, California
WILLIAM KEATING, Massachusetts
DAVID CICILLINE, Rhode Island
ALAN GRAYSON, Florida
AMI BERA, California
ALAN S. LOWENTHAL, California
GRACE MENG, New York
LOIS FRANKEL, Florida
TULSI GABBARD, Hawaii
JOAQUIN CASTRO, Texas
ROBIN L. KELLY, Illinois
BRENDAN F. BOYLE, Pennsylvania

AMY PORTER, *Chief of Staff*   THOMAS SHEEHY, *Staff Director*
JASON STEINBAUM, *Democratic Staff Director*

————

SUBCOMMITTEE ON TERRORISM, NONPROLIFERATION, AND TRADE

TED POE, Texas, *Chairman*

JOE WILSON, South Carolina
DARRELL E. ISSA, California
PAUL COOK, California
SCOTT PERRY, Pennsylvania
REID J. RIBBLE, Wisconsin
LEE M. ZELDIN, New York

WILLIAM KEATING, Massachusetts
BRAD SHERMAN, California
BRIAN HIGGINS, New York
JOAQUIN CASTRO, Texas
ROBIN L. KELLY, Illinois

CONTENTS

WITNESSES

LETTERS, STATEMENTS, ETC., SUBMITTED FOR THE HEARING

APPENDIX

BOKO HARAM: THE ISLAMIST INSURGENCY IN WEST AFRICA

WEDNESDAY, FEBRUARY 24, 2016

House of Representatives,
Subcommittee on Terrorism, Nonproliferation, and Trade,
Committee on Foreign Affairs,
Washington, DC.

The subcommittee met, pursuant to notice, at 2 o'clock p.m., in room 2200 Rayburn House Office Building, Hon. Ted Poe (chairman of the subcommittee) presiding.

Mr. POE. The subcommittee will come to order. Without objection, all members may have 5 days to submit statements, questions, and extraneous materials for the record subject to the length limitation in the rules. I will make my opening statement at this time.

Boko Haram has killed thousands throughout its reign of terror in Nigeria and neighboring countries. They strap bombs to little girls and send them into public markets to act as suicide bombers. On the screen in front of each member and the panel, there is a map of Nigeria. There are mostly Christians in the south, Muslims in the north, and while the vast oil reserves prop up the economy of the country, the economy in the north is bad. It has little natural resources, has bad infrastructure, some say lots of corruption.

For years, the north has felt neglected. So when Boko Haram started in 2002 it was able to tap into that sense of disenfranchisement and frustration with government. Boko Haram means ''Western education is sinful.'' The goal is to create an Islamic caliphate in West Africa along the lines of ISIS' caliphate in Iraq and Syria, and they will violently do anything to achieve the goal.

Boko Haram, like ISIS, tell Christians to convert or die. Christian women are forced to marry them and convert to Islam. Christians have seen their schools burned to the ground, some schools burned to the ground with the children inside. Their homes are targeted, their churches are destroyed because they are Christians. We all remember the kidnapping of close to 300 schoolgirls, now almost 2 years ago, in April 2014. Many of those girls were reportedly forced to convert to Islam and they are still missing. There are growing concerns that Boko Haram might have forced some of these girls to carry out suicide attacks.

Throughout 2014, the terrorist group successfully seized huge amounts of territory in northeastern Nigeria. Most of us are not familiar with how big Nigeria is, but Boko Haram is holding territory roughly the size of Belgium. To take in more territory, Boko Haram killed by the thousands, in 2014, Boko Haram killed nearly 7,000 people—murdered is a better word than killed—making them the deadliest terrorist group in the world, even surpassing ISIS.

Boko Haram pledged allegiance to ISIS in 2015 and rebranded its state as the Islamic State's West Africa Province. Boko Haram has overextended itself, however, when it tried to hold territory in Nigeria and other West African militaries were destroying it in 2015. Boko Haram was forced to give up on holding territory, but it has not been defeated. Boko Haram is still capable of launching deadly attacks throughout the Lake Chad Basin. My staff has tracked these attacks. There is hardly a day that goes by that there is not some sort of Boko Haram attack that kills innocent people.

Over the past few years, relations between Nigeria and the United States have been strained. Joint military trainings were cancelled and the U.S. hesitated to supply weapons to Nigeria's military citing other concerns about human rights abuses. The United States took 11 years to designate Boko Haram as a foreign terrorist organization, then on November 12th, 2013, ironically, the night before this subcommittee and the African Subcommittee had a joint hearing on Boko Haram on why it was not on the FTO list, State Department called to say it was going to designate the organization and put them on the Foreign Terrorist Organization list.

That is an important step, but there are questions about the implementation of the designation. It does not seem that all the tools that this designation carries are being brought to bear on the group, especially when it comes to stopping the financing of Boko Haram.

The United States has started to do more to help Nigeria combat Boko Haram since the election of Nigerian President Buhari in May 2015. Infantry training has restarted and we are seeing an increased level of cooperation between AFRICOM and Nigerian military. In October, the administration announced that it was sending troops and drones to Cameroon as well as surveillance aircraft to Niger, but like the FTO designation, these are steps that should have been taken years ago before Boko Haram was allowed to murder more people than ISIS.

We must do more to support our African partners to stamp out this Islamic radical menace once and for all. The fighting against Boko Haram is essential to U.S. national security interests. In ISIS, we have already seen what happens when we underestimate a terrorist group. Boko Haram may not have the capability to attack the United States today, but neither did al-Qaeda in the years prior to 9/11. This hearing will help expose this deadly assault Boko Haram has committed against civilized peoples, and I will yield to the ranking member, Mr. Keating, from Massachusetts.

Mr. KEATING. Thank you, Mr. Chairman, for conducting this important hearing, and I would like to thank our witnesses for being here today as well.

While it was the heinous and vicious kidnapping in 2014 of 276 schoolgirls from their dormitory in Chibok that first brought Boko Haram to the attention of much of the world, we know all too well that this group is responsible for the deaths of thousands of men, women and children since 2003. In fact, in 2014 alone, Boko Haram was responsible for approximately 7,000 deaths which is higher than the amount attributed to ISIL. ISIL killed, by comparison, 6,073 in 2014.

In order to study, understand, and successfully combat Boko Haram, I believe we should view and respond to them as both an insurgency and as a terrorist organization. At its heart, Boko Haram is fed on the poverty, unemployment and disenfranchisement in the northeast part of Nigeria and surrounding areas as well, accumulating territory and widening its influence. The northeastern regions where Boko Haram has celebrated significant territorial gains is largely Muslim and trails the southern part of the country, which is largely Christian, in the scope of education and wealth.

Since its establishment, Boko Haram has existed to marginalize Nigeria's Muslim population and delegitimize its government. Recent years have borne witness to its graduation from smaller rudimentary attacks to targeting Nigerian Government to a full scale assault on Westernization and governance in Nigeria as well, with both Muslims and Christians among the victims of Boko Haram's terrorism.

Since 2009, Boko Haram has played a direct harmful role in destabilizing Nigeria. Its violent campaign against the government has left parts of the country in ruins. Nearly 1 year ago, in early March 2015, Boko Haram's leader pledged allegiance to the Islamic State which led to the creation of the Islamic State's West Africa Province. Boko Haram has long been linked to other terrorist organizations in Africa, including al-Qaeda, and this shift in the allegiance could be interpreted as a quest for increased recruitment and fundraising opportunities.

It is clear that Boko Haram's activities are at the heart of a broader regional crisis. The group has expanded its operations into neighboring Cameroon, Chad, Niger, and since 2014, these countries have increasingly been subject to attacks by this group. This instability has led to unprecedented food shortages and child malnutrition. According to the United Nations, more than 5.6 million people are facing a food crisis in Nigeria and bordering countries.

While there has been more than successful efforts at the local level and efforts to combat Boko Haram, much work is still needed to restore peace and provide for the millions of people impacted by this devastation. This includes internal efforts to root out corruption within the government and military, protect and advance cooperation on human rights practices, and to revitalize subjugated regions within the country as well as establishing a Multinational Joint Task Force to combat the threat of the Islamist insurgency in West Africa.

Finally, I am grateful for the work of many of my colleagues led by Africa, Global Health, Global Human Rights, and International Organizations' groups as well, Subcommittee Ranking Member Karen Bass of California, Nigerian Caucus Chair Sheila Jackson Lee, and Representative Frederica Wilson, who advanced the regional strategy to eliminate the threat of Boko Haram and provide humanitarian relief to the affected regions. All three of these congresswomen have personally met with Nigerian officials and even traveled to the region to raise awareness through Bring Back Our Girls campaign.

4

These efforts have made real gains in promoting equal access to education, economic opportunity for women and girls, and I look forward to hearing from our witnesses today on existing efforts by the Nigerian Government and regional task force where there must be increased focus and increased attention. Thank you, Mr. Chairman. I yield back.

Mr. POE. Mr. Higgins, do you want to make an opening statement?

Mr. HIGGINS. I am good. Go to the panel.

Mr. POE. All right. So without objection, all the witnesses' prepared statements will be made part of the record. I ask that each witness keep their presentation to no more than 5 minutes. And just so you know, it is going to get cooler in here because the expert just showed up.

I will introduce each witness and give them time for opening statements. Jennifer Cooke is the director of the Africa Program at the Center for Strategic and International Studies. She also manages a range of projects on political, economic and security dynamics in Africa.

Ms. Alice Hunt Friend is an adjunct senior fellow at the Center for New American Security. She previously served as the principal director for African Affairs in OSD Policy where she focused primarily on Libya, South Sudan and the Great Lakes region.

Dr. Daveed Gartenstein-Ross is a senior fellow at the Foundation for Defense and Democracies. We thank him for substituting for Mr. Jacob Zenn who is unable to make it from Nigeria, and especially the short notice that you came in on. Dr. Gartenstein-Ross did not provide a written testimony but will speak to us about Boko Haram broader counterterrorism issues in Africa.

Ms. Cooke, we will start with you and you have 5 minutes.

STATEMENT OF MS. JENNIFER G. COOKE, DIRECTOR, AFRICA PROGRAM, CENTER FOR INTERNATIONAL AND STRATEGIC STUDIES

Ms. COOKE. Thank you, Mr. Chairman and Ranking Member Keating and members of the subcommittee. Thank you very much for the opportunity to testify today on Boko Haram. This hearing could not be more timely or important. My testimony today draws substantially on recent travel in January to Maiduguri in northeast Nigeria, to Abuja and Niamey, and earlier travel to Northern Mali and Senegal.

I would like to make two broad points. The first is on the urgency of the situation. Why is it such an important moment for the United States to engage and amplify its support against Boko Haram, and second, what should be some of the priority areas for U.S. support.

So why the urgency? Nigeria and the governments of the region have unquestionably made important progress against Boko Haram. The group is largely being routed from territorial control, thousands of members and a number of its senior leaders have been captured or killed, thousands of women and girls have been rescued from brutal captivity, and the groups media operation, significant weapon in the terrorist arsenal, has gone largely quiet. That progress is real. It should be acknowledged and supported.

But it is cold comfort for the victims and families of Boko Haram's most recent attacks and the many communities and displaced persons in northeast Nigeria and the broader Lake Chad Basin region. These communities remain vulnerable to asymmetrical attacks, and eliminating the capacity for these attacks would be much more difficult than a territorial rout.

The regional and global context makes this an even more critical moment for decisive action to prevent Boko Haram from regenerating or a successor group from taking its place. Every effort should be made to ensure that the Lake Chad region and the Sahel, more broadly, do not become proxy battleground for al-Qaeda and ISIL or broader ideological coalitions.

Boko Haram and other Sahelian extremist groups have a long record of dynamism and opportunism. Alliance amongst these groups that include training, weaponry tactics are dangerous, but growing rivalries between them could prove equally dangerous. Boko Haram, as you have said, pledged allegiance to ISIL last year. At the same time, al-Qaeda's Sahelian affiliates, al-Qaeda in the Islamic Maghreb, al-Mourabitoun and others, have reasserted themselves with high profile attacks in Bamako and Ouagadougou. After being temporarily on the defensive and losing ground to the ISIL brand, the quest for notoriety and one-upmanship among these various jihadist groups will have tragic human costs.

The entrenchment of ISIL in Libya adds to the urgency. ISIL's rising profile right now is a magnet for many fighters. Security forces have intercepted militants traveling from Nigeria, Niger, Chad, Mali, into Libya and we know that some have successfully managed to get to the front lines. Political stabilization and military intervention against ISIL in Libya may be good for Libya, but it will almost certainly drive these fighters back out into the region more battle hardened, better armed, and more ruthless than before.

I am going to quickly move to priorities, areas for engagement. We know that a long term, comprehensive approach that puts economic opportunity and education at the center will be important, but it is not the time for that. We don't have the degree of normalcy that allows that. Those need to be started with urgency, but we need some immediate steps before that can fully happen.

Help prevent Boko Haram from regenerating. Essential to preventing regeneration of Boko Haram will be cooperation among Nigeria and its regional neighbors to block supply routes and exfiltration, eradicate rear bases and training camps, and share intelligence on movements of weaponry and supplies. The Multinational Joint Task Force is being riven by rivalries and recriminations. U.S. has to pressure those countries to come together for genuine cooperation.

Blocking the financial supply routes, critically important. U.S. should mobilize significant resources to this end through the Department of Treasury's Terrorist Financing Tracking Program, building the capacity of Nigeria and others to do the same.

Third is to support an off ramp for Boko Haram fighters that makes surrender a more attractive option. They are not all there for their own will. Many of are being coerced, many including women are being kidnapped and indoctrinated. The U.S. State Department and USAID should support Nigerian efforts to help sort these many fighters, fast track them through a judicial process and provide programming for reintegration, deradicalization where possible.

The second big area is to support civilian protection and welfare. We have to support the capacity and professionalism of regional forces—more engagement not less. I know that human rights abuses by the Nigerian military have been a sticking point in U.S.-Nigerian military engagement. The U.S. Government should continue to press for accountability, but it should also recognize that appropriate training and equipment can help mitigate the possibility of human rights abuse. As Nigerian troops have become more competent and better equipped, incidents of abuse have diminished. Boko Haram has killed more civilians in the last year than ISIL and it is not a good time to deny regional forces the access to the critical equipment that they need.

My final point is to support internally displaced people and Boko Haram surviving victims. Some 3 million people in the region have been displaced because of Boko Haram. The vast majority are in Nigeria, but in the surrounding region as well. There is little certainty on when they will be able to return to their homes. The international community along with Nigerian Government and citizens need to rally to support these displaced communities ensuring that the many children among them are given the education and services they need to thrive and to eventually help rebuild the northeast region.

Finally, the fate of these 219 girls kidnapped by Chibok remains an enduring and tragic mystery and the effort to locate and recover them should be sustained and supporting. But there are thousands of girls and women who have escaped and been rescued from captivity who have endured unthinkable brutality and trauma and they should not be neglected. The U.S. Government and indeed the American people should support and amplify the efforts of Nigeria and the region to give these survivors the psychosocial, economic and moral support that they very well deserve. Thank you very much. I will leave it at that and welcome your questions.

[The prepared statement of Ms. Cooke follows:]

Statement before the House Foreign Affairs Committee
Subcommittee on Terrorism, Nonproliferation, and Trade

"Boko Haram: The Islamist Insurgency in West Africa"

Statement by Jennifer G. Cooke
Director, Africa Program
Center for Strategic and International Studies (CSIS)

February 24, 2016
Rayburn House Office Building

Mr. Chairman, Ranking Member Keating, and distinguished members of the Subcommittee, I would like to thank you for the invitation to testify at today's hearing, "Boko Haram: the Islamist Insurgency in West Africa," which could not be more timely or important.

My name is Jennifer Cooke, and I direct the Africa Program at the Center for Strategic and International Studies (CSIS), a bipartisan, nonprofit organization based in Washington, D.C. Political, economic. and security dynamics in Nigeria have been a priority focus of my work with the CSIS Africa Program over the last 15 years: from insurgency in the country's oil-producing Niger Delta, to energy sector reform, health service delivery, the fight against corruption, electoral politics, and the early emergence of Boko Haram. I have traveled extensively within Nigeria and the broader West African sub-region. My testimony today reflects findings from a trip in January of this year to Abuja and Maiduguri, the birthplace of Boko Haram, and to Niamey, Niger, as part of a CSIS project on violent extremism in the Sahel. I've also recently traveled to Senegal and Northern Mali as part of this project. My remarks and written testimony represent my views and not those of my colleagues or of CSIS as an institution.

Mr. Chairman, recent assaults against unprotected civilian populations in North East Nigeria, northern Cameroon, and Niger are a stark illustration of Boko Haram's enduring lethality and the terrible human cost of the asymmetrical incursions—suicide bombings and "hit and run" attacks, improvised explosive devices—that have been its enduring tactical mainstay. In late January, Boko Haram militants launched a particularly brutal assault on Dalori, a village on the outskirts of the Borno State capital of Maiduguri in North East Nigeria, detonating suicide vests and fire-bombing houses while occupants, including many children, were trapped within. The Dalori attack left some 85 people dead. Just a few weeks later, two female suicide bombers killed more than 60 people in a camp for internally displaced persons (IDPs) in the Borno town of Dikwa. A third would-be assailant in that attack, a teenage girl strapped with explosives, had a last minute change of heart, confessing that she did not want to kill her parents, who were residents of the camp. Little more than a week later, in the village of Mémé in northern Cameroon, two militants detonated explosives hidden in the village's drinking water supplies, killing themselves and 20 people and leaving many more injured.

Boko Haram has been significantly weakened over the last 18 months, as a more robust and concerted effort by the Nigerian military—in partnership with security forces in neighboring Chad, Cameroon, and Niger—has routed the group from territories that it controlled and significantly degraded its capabilities and leadership. Many thousands of Boko Haram members, along with a number of its senior leaders, have been killed or captured, and the group no longer appears to have access to the kinds of transport and equipment—tanks, armored vehicles, Toyota Hilux trucks—that it has had in the past. Regional forces have continued to destroy Boko Haram camps and rear bases; the

Nigerian Air Force has been engaged in a sustained assault on Boko Haram redoubts in Sambisa Forest, taking out fuel pumps, solar panels, and weapons caches. Regional military forces have rescued thousands of women and girls who had been kidnapped by Boko Haram members and held in the most appalling of circumstances. The group's media operation—which reportedly received technical assistance from ISIL—has gone largely quiet, and there have been no video appearances by erstwhile leader Abubakar Shekau (or by any of his alleged imposters) since early 2015. These advances against Boko Haram are real: they should be acknowledged and supported by the United States and international community. But this progress is cold comfort for the victims and families of Boko Haram's most recent attacks and the many communities of North East Nigeria and the Lake Chad Basin region who remain vulnerable to the group's continuing predations.

The fight against Boko Haram is far from over. The group's strength was never as an organized fighting force, but rather as a fractured, ruthless organization, willing to inflict maximum damage on the softest of targets—school children, marketplaces, mosques, and churches. Eliminating the capacity for these attacks will be far more difficult than territorial rout.

Further—and one reason that today's hearing is so important—it is important to remember that Boko Haram has proved resilient to setbacks in the past. The possibility that it will regroup and rebuild should be the source of critical regional and international concern. In the current global and regional context, where jihadist groups compete for notoriety and ISIL entrenches its presence in Libya, there is an urgent need to prevent Boko Haram from regenerating and possibly coming back more virulent, destructive, and globally connected than before.

First steps in the long road ahead.

There is broad consensus among policymakers and analysts that for sustained security against Boko Haram and possible successor groups over the long term, regional governments will need to plan—and, when possible, rapidly implement— comprehensive strategies that improve socioeconomic conditions for impoverished and marginalized communities. Infrastructure development, economic revitalization, transparent and accountable governance, and an end to corruption are all high on the priority list. At the center of that longer-term strategy must be a major effort to provide the region's youthful populations with improved access to quality education and economic opportunity. But these longer-term strategies, even if started with urgency, will take time to bear fruit, and they are predicated on a level of security and normalcy that today does not exist. Counting on a comprehensive development and governance approach to secure the peace is not realistic right now, but neither is a purely military effort to "destroy" Boko Haram.

There are three priority areas that warrant United States support:

Prevent Boko Haram from regenerating.

Boko Haram has proved resilient in the past, and constraining its ability to regroup or resupply itself by drawing on regional networks and transport corridors is critical. Boko Haram members have always been able to move with ease across Nigeria's northern borders: to Chad (via Lake Chad and its many islands), to Niger, and through the heavily forested and mountainous areas that straddle the Nigeria-Cameroon border. Following the extrajudicial killing of founder Mohammed Yusuf in 2009, much of Boko Haram's leadership fled Nigeria across these porous northern frontiers. During that hiatus, Abubakar Shekau is said to have traveled to northern Mali and trained with the Movement for Unity and Jihad in West Africa (MUJAO); other members reportedly traveled through Chad and Niger to train and fight alongside jihadist elements in Somalia, Algeria, and Afghanistan. They returned to Nigeria in 2010, and Boko Haram reemerged as a far more deadly and sophisticated enterprise. Turmoil in Libya and the fall of Muammar el-Qaddafi in 2011 resulted in an additional influx of weaponry from Libyan arsenals and of Nigerian fighters (many Nigerians were members of Qaddafi's security forces), arriving primarily through supply routes in Chad.

Today, as ISIL expands operations in Libya, it will likely become a magnet for Boko Haram fighters driven out by Nigerian, Chadian, Nigerien and Cameroonian forces. This may appear to offer some respite to the Lake Chad Basin region, but if international moves against ISIL in Libya are eventually successful, those fighters are almost certain to return, and the possibility of an even more sophisticated, battle-hardened, and ruthless Islamist insurgency should be an issue of grave concern.

Sustain diplomatic pressure for more effective regional cooperation.

Essential to preventing regeneration of Boko Haram will be cooperation among Nigeria and its regional neighbors to block supply routes and exfiltration, eradicate rear-bases and training camps, and share intelligence on movements of fighters and on sources of funding and supply. The regional Multinational Joint Task Force (MNJTF), which comprises Benin, Cameroon, Chad, Niger, and Nigeria, was established to do just that. The task force has largely stalled, however, as distrust and mutual recriminations between Chad and Nigeria persist, and as differences in perceptions of threat, responsibility, and priority are hampering progress. Less than half of the task force's estimated $700 million budget has been raised, and both Chad and Nigeria—where oil exports are the primary source of government revenues—are in fiscal crisis. Key diplomatic and security partners—including the United States, France, the African Union, and United Nations—should intensify the push for more robust regional cooperation and ensure that those efforts are adequately and appropriately funded.

Assist in disrupting Boko Haram's financial lifelines.

As important as blocking the physical ingress and egress of fighters and weapons from the region will be a transnational, coordinated effort to track and disrupt Boko Haram's domestic and international sources of finance. The U.S. government, through the Treasury Department's Terrorist Financing Tracking Program, is uniquely positioned to assist in this regard and should mobilize significant support and technical assistance to expand the capacity of Nigeria's Financial Intelligence Unit. Nigerian President Muhammadu Buhari has expressed his commitment to uncovering and pursuing Boko Haram's financial sponsors, and the United States, in partnership with regional and international law enforcement agencies and financial institutions, can play an important role in helping Nigeria and its neighbors map and disrupt terror these flows.

Support an off-ramp for Boko Haram fighters.

An important part of weakening Boko Haram and undermining its ability to regenerate will be to establish a process that makes surrender a more attractive option for current members. Boko Haram members are not an undifferentiated mass: within the group's ranks are hard-line ideologues and criminal opportunists, leaders and followers, adults and children. Many were forcibly conscripted; others (including many girls and women) were kidnapped and subsequently indoctrinated; some joined for economic gain or a sense of empowerment. Even those members who were coerced into joining—or were underage—may feel "stuck" in the group, unable to return to their communities and fearful of being killed if they surrender. Many may see embedding themselves further within the group—or fleeing to Libya—as their only option. Nigeria's National Security Agency has established prison-based de-radicalization and reeducation programs, although funding and political support for the programs are weak. Nigeria will need to rapidly expand the absorptive capacity of these programs, which could also provide an important source of insight and evidence for CVE programming in Nigeria and beyond. The U.S. State Department and USAID should provide support, profile, and much-needed technical assistance for these programs, particularly in building capacities for psychosocial support, and should strongly encourage similar programs in Chad, Niger, and Cameroon.

Enhance capacities for civilian protection and welfare.

Civilian populations in North East Nigeria and the Lake Chad region remain acutely vulnerable to asymmetrical attacks by Boko Haram and to the hardship and uncertainty of displacement. Both regional security forces and civilian leaders will need to give much greater priority to civilian protection and engagement and win back the trust of communities that have suffered from decades of underinvestment and marginalization. This will require a change in mindset as well as improved capacity to deliver security and services.

Support the capacity and professionalism of regional security forces.

Preventing and responding to asymmetrical attacks across wide swathes of sparsely populated territory and pursuing increasingly fragmented and nimble cohorts of militants will remain a daunting challenge. Security forces in the region will need the equipment and materiel that allows them to collect and communicate intelligence on a real time basis, deploy quickly, and target militants with greater precision. Training by U.S. and other international partners can help build these specialized capacities and transform regional militaries into forces more capable of countering current threats.

Human rights abuses by the Nigerian military have been a sticking point in U.S.-Nigerian military engagement. Nigerian forces, ill-prepared, poorly equipped, and overwhelmed by an unprecedented threat, were responsible for a series of egregious abuses and use of disproportionate force as the insurgency intensified in 2011. President Buhari, in his inaugural address, pledged to investigate allegations of abuse and hold those found to have committed abuses to account, and the bilateral relationship appears to have gotten a fresh start. The U.S. government should continue to press for accountability, but it should also recognize that appropriate training and equipment can help mitigate the possibility of human rights abuse. As Nigerian troops have become more competent and better-equipped, incidents of abuse in the fight against Boko Haram have diminished. Boko Haram has killed more civilians in the last year than ISIL, and it is not a good time to deny regional forces access to the critical equipment they need. Armored vehicles, protective gear, state of the art technologies, and aircraft that allow rapid deployment and precision targeting will be important tools in stopping Boko Haram attacks and in giving confidence and improving the morale of forces on the front line.

Support the internally displaced and Boko Haram's surviving victims.

Some three million people in the Lake Chad region have been displaced because of Boko Haram, the vast majority within Nigeria, but with significant displacements in Cameroon and Niger as well. A small fraction live within government-sponsored camps; others have had to fend for themselves, melding into host communities or informal settlements. With insecurity and violence likely to persist, the needs of these citizens— whether they live in camps or not—will remain an urgent challenge. In 2015, some 450 children in Borno State IDP camps died of malnutrition, according to the State Emergency Management Agency. Many IDPs have been deeply traumatized and are— with good reason—wary of returning to their homes. In many cases there is little for them to go home to: villages and towns, homes, wells, and infrastructure have been destroyed. The majority of IDPs have little certainty as to when they might be able to return home, and there is a possibility that many will live in this displaced limbo for years to come. The international community, along with the Nigerian government and citizens, should rally to support these displaced communities, ensuring that the many children among them are given the education and services they need to thrive and eventually help rebuild the North East region.

Boko Haram's many thousands of victims will need continued support and some possibility of a return to normalcy. The fate of at least 219 girls kidnapped in Chibok remains an enduring and tragic mystery, and the effort to locate and recover them should be sustained and supported. But the many girls and women who have escaped or been rescued from captivity—who have endured unthinkable brutality and trauma—should not be neglected. The U.S. government—and indeed the American people—should support and amplify the efforts of Nigeria and the region to give these survivors the psychosocial, economic, and moral support they deserve.

Improve community engagement and strategic communication.

As Boko Haram reverts primarily to asymmetrical tactics, collaboration and timely exchange of information between security forces and communities takes on paramount importance. Building trust with communities, many of which have never benefited from government service or protection, will be a long-term process, but expanding mechanisms of communication and building the basis for an eventual culture of community policing should be an urgent priority. The U.S. government and international community should support strategic communication strategies and encourage the timely and consistent provision of information and messaging to affected communities.

Think beyond Boko Haram: consider jihadist rivalries and alliances.

U.S. policymakers must consider Boko Haram in a broader global and regional context. The Sahel region, including the Lake Chad Basin, risks becoming a proxy battleground for larger ideological and geopolitical rivalries. Competition between ISIL and al Qaeda, Shiites and Sunnis—even between Iran and Saudi Arabia—could fuel increasingly deadly competition among Islamist extremist groups of the region.

Boko Haram and other Sahelian extremist groups have a long record of dynamism and opportunism. Internal disputes over ideology, ego, strategy, and leadership—and competition for profile, manpower, and resources—have ensured a continual fracturing and reforming of alliances and rivalries among them. Today, mounting rivalry between ISIL and al Qaeda could raise the stakes for jihadist competition even further. Boko Haram pledged allegiance to ISIL last year, renaming itself Islamic State West Africa Province. At the same time, al Qaeda's Sahel affiliates—Al Qaeda in the Islamic Maghreb (AQIM), MUJAO, al Mourabitoun, and others—have reasserted themselves with high-profile attacks in Bamako and Ouagadougou, after being temporarily on the defensive following the French-led intervention into Mali. The quest for notoriety and one-upmanship among jihadist groups will have heavy and tragic human costs.

Compounding the possibility of sectarian and ideological competition is the rising assertiveness of Nigeria's Shiite movement. In November, Boko Haram claimed an attack against members of the Islamic Movement of Nigeria (IMN), the country's largest Shiite organization, as they marched in an annual pilgrimage. Just weeks later in

December, the Nigerian military killed hundreds of IMN members (the group claims as many as 700) in the North Central town of Zaria, flattening the movement's central mosque and gravely wounding its charismatic leader Ibrahim al-Zakzaky, who remains in detention. The government has remained largely silent on the real reasons for the massacre, but in private, federal officials hint at a serious and imminent threat from elements within organization, which to date has publicly professed a policy of nonviolence. An ongoing investigation may provide greater clarity on the nature of the threat and the circumstances of the assault, but many observers worry that the brutality of the military response could serve only to inflame and further radicalize Shiite elements, very much as the killing of Yusuf and his followers in 2009 generated a more vicious and violent iteration of Boko Haram.

A number of Nigerian analysts express concern that the Zaria incident—as well as the al Qaeda-ISIL rivalry—could draw Nigeria into a broader geopolitical and ideological contest. President Hassan Rouhani of Iran spoke to President Buhari following the Zaria killings, expressing his concern for the country's Shiite community and dismay that al-Zakzaky remained in detention. King Salman of Saudi Arabia called President Buhari shortly thereafter, reportedly expressing his support and pledging greater cooperation in the fight against terror.

There will be no decisive victory in the long fight against Boko Haram. With the group now largely routed from the towns it controlled, the security situation in some ways has returned to where it was before Boko Haram developed territorial ambitions. But this should not be cause for complacency. In fact, this is an important opportunity to urgently block its capacity and opportunity to regenerate and to insulate the region from possible spillover from Libyan turmoil. The U.S. has a strong interest in fortifying the countries of the region against this possibility and laying the groundwork for the much bigger task of economic revitalization and recovery.

Mr. POE. Well, you are going to get those in a minute.

Ms. Friend, I recognize you for your opening statement. Thank you.

STATEMENT OF MS. ALICE HUNT FRIEND, ADJUNCT SENIOR FELLOW, CENTER FOR NEW AMERICAN SECURITY

Ms. FRIEND. Thank you, Chairman Poe. Chairman Poe, Ranking Member Keating, members of the subcommittee, it is an honor to be here today to participate in the important ongoing discussion of the threat Boko Haram poses to Nigeria and the wider West African region. Throughout its almost 14-year history, Boko Haram has proven to be a ruthless and resilient organization, and it is wise to continue taking the threat the group poses seriously despite its recent setbacks.

Since early 2015, Nigeria, joined by a multinational coalition has prosecuted an offensive against Boko Haram that has deprived the group of its territorial control and degraded its capacity to confront national security forces directly. This is the second retreat for the group since 2002 and demonstrates its comparative weakness when confronted with a well organized and determined military force.

In an insurgency, however, the offense often has the advantage. Battered but undeterred, Boko Haram has turned again to asymmetric tactics and a rich array of targets. The group terrorizes public spaces that are notoriously difficult to secure such as markets and transit depots, attacks often feature multiple coordinated bombings and increasingly rely on kidnapped women and girls wearing suicide vests. These strikes have succeeded in reestablishing the group's pre-2015 daily tempo of casualties, killing and injuring upwards of 50 to 100 people in an average attack. A mix of attacks on urban and rural areas gives the population a sense that there is no refuge from Boko Haram's reign of terror.

Despite their continued ability to menace daily life in the northeast, just how large and capable the group is today compared to late 2014 is difficult to assess. Boko Haram's remaining members seem to be scattered throughout the Nigerian countryside and the border regions with Chad, Niger, and Cameroon. Their use of kidnapped women to exercise suicide attacks, while tactically advantageous, also suggests a shrunken supply of adult male foot soldiers. The group has been reduced to ambushes along rural roads in lieu of territorial control.

Perhaps as a way to distract from its battlefield losses, in March of last year Boko Haram's leader, Abubakar Shekau, publicly declared the group's allegiance to the Islamic State. The practical effect of this allegiance is unclear so far. There is some evidence that the Islamic State may have attempted to support earlier improvements to Boko Haram's media campaign, but there are fewer signs of financial support of capacity building flowing to the West African affiliate. Some analysts speculate that the alliance largely served propaganda purposes for both groups making the Islamic State look like it was expanding even under intense pressure in the Middle East, and making Boko Haram look relevant to the global Islamist terrorist network.

Upon his election in 2015, Nigeria's new President, Muhammadu Buhari, pledged to defeat Boko Haram by the end of the year and took several actions to advance toward this goal including ostensibly increasing resources for military personnel after years of underinvestment. At the same time, the Buhari administration has announced renewed efforts to investigate and prosecute military violations of human rights and corruption. It is unclear how far these anti-corruption efforts aimed at the security services will truly go, but Buhari's efforts to date represent long overdue steps in the right direction.

Nigeria's revitalization of its counterterrorism operations has been aided by a regional and international push for collaboration to combat the threat. In the wake of the Chibok schoolgirl kidnappings in 2014, Benin, Chad, Cameroon, Niger and Nigeria agreed to reactivate a longstanding but disused Multinational Joint Task Force structure. The MNJTF's tasks include targeted operations against Boko Haram, capturing members of the terrorist group, border security, recovery of abductees, regional coordination and intelligence sharing. Unfortunately, the MNJTF has had an uneven start with budget and troop shortfalls and limited coordination efforts leading to questions about the task force's sustainability.

Task force members focus largely on their own border regions and it is unclear how much tactical, operational, or strategic level coordination actually occurs. Nevertheless, real operational gains have resulted from the combined, if not entirely coordinated, efforts. Just yesterday, for example, Nigerian and Cameroonian forces carried out a successful joint operation that reportedly resulted in 20 Boko Haram casualties and a rescue of 150 captives.

Beyond these immediate security efforts, the conflict has displaced upwards of 2 million people, many of whom are children. This glut of refugees and the challenges behind reintegrating former Boko Haram captives indicate a humanitarian and social crisis that may long outlast the fighting.

In this context, the Nigerian Government must take a strong lead in developing the political will and financial commitment to provide holistic security in areas ravaged by Boko Haram. Such a security plan should include an effective policing capacity to protect the population and deny Boko Haram's successful attacks coupled with ongoing military operations to keep the terrorists on the defensive. Both forces should be bolstered by intelligence capabilities and linked to an efficient justice sector able to conduct detention operations and swift prosecutions according to international legal standards.

All of this must be coupled with a robust development program that can provide basic services and infrastructure to long neglected communities. Nigeria does not have to do this work on its own. International assistance including from the United States offers a deep well of resources and expertise to the government and Boko Haram's victims.

Nigeria is a beneficiary of multiple U.S. security assistance programs through which the U.S. has recently provided communications gear, equipment and armored vehicles. The U.S. also supports efforts by other regional partners to combat Boko Haram including Niger and Cameroon, and frequently consults with European partners to coordinate efforts and share information. This broad approach ensures that the counter-Boko Haram effort is a diversified and sustainable portfolio of investment in regional and international partners.

But it is important to remember that international support efforts can only proceed at the pace set by Nigeria. The U.S. recently restarted infantry battalion training after a long hiatus with plans to build on such engagements and ongoing evaluations of Nigerian equipment requests. Continued accusations of human rights violations by Nigerian security forces and Nigerians' own concerns about protecting its sovereignty mean that all external support is preceded with careful and mutual evaluations of both sides' intentions. These engagements are complex but must continue in order to sustain pressure on Boko Haram. The U.S. and other Nigerian partners should continue to point out the connections between government conduct in the north and the resilience and support of the local communities sustaining an upper hand against Boko Haram. Thank you, and I look forward to your questions.

[The prepared statement of Ms. Friend follows:]

Center for a
New American
Security

February 24, 2016

Testimony before the House Foreign Affairs Committee, Subcommittee on Terrorism, Nonproliferation, and Trade

Boko Haram: The Islamist Insurgency in West Africa

Alice Hunt Friend, Adjunct Senior Fellow
Center for a New American Security

Boko Haram's Origins and Evolution

Boko Haram began as a religious-political movement in Borno State in northeastern Nigeria around 2002. Led by a man named Mohammed Yusuf and operating largely out of a mosque he founded in the regional capital, Maiduguri, the group advocated a return to shari'a, or Islamic law, and a rejection of secularism and corruption in public and private life. Focused on targets in Nigeria, they began to use violence to punish Muslims they deemed were indulging in apostasy, often relying on brief hit-and-run tactics using light arms and traveling by car or motorcycle.[1] These attacks attracted police attention, and over the next several years, the group's engagement with law enforcement escalated into ever-deadlier exchanges. The violence spread into neighboring Nigerian states and culminated in a conflagration in 2009 that left Yusuf and several hundred of his adherents dead, and hundreds more captured by police.

The group seemed to be in full retreat, and was inactive for almost a year until Yusuf's second-in-command, Abubakar bin Mohammad Shekau, released a video and a manifesto announcing his leadership of Boko Haram and threatening revenge on the Nigerian state as well as its Western backers. Often expressing common cause with al Qaeda, at the end of 2010 and the beginning of 2011 the group launched a series of improvised explosive device (IED) attacks against government installations, religious leaders, and politicians. In mid-June, the group executed the first suicide bombing attack inside Nigeria against the police Inspector-General, and in August it launched another suicide bombing against the UN offices in the country's capital, Abuja.[2] Attacks escalated through 2013 and 2014, when Boko Haram expanded its array of targets, frequently engaged Nigerian forces directly, and overran border towns and increasing swaths of Nigerian territory. The attacks became numbing in their

---

[1] J. Peter Pham, "How Boko Haram Became the Islamic State's West Africa Province," *The Journal of International Security Affairs*, Winter, 2016.

[2] Senan Murray and Adam Nossiter, "Suicide Bomber Attacks UN Building in Nigeria," *The New York Times*, August

frequency, claiming 70 lives one day, 19 the next, 21 the day after.[3] The group was so successful at cowing security forces and terrorizing local populations that Shekau declared it had enough territorial control to have established a "caliphate" in northern Nigeria.[4]

As Boko Haram's capacity expanded, it absorbed more and more local people into its ranks, many of them unwilling victims. Young boys were conscripted into service while girls were kidnapped and used or sold as sex slaves and domestic workers.[5] Most famously, in April of 2014 Boko Haram kidnapped almost 300 schoolgirls from the town of Chibok, more than 200 of whom have never been recovered.

By the end of 2014, Boko Haram had earned the dubious honor of being called the world's deadliest terror group by the Institute for Economics and Peace. In its 2015 report on global terrorism, the IEP noted that in 2014, Nigeria "witnessed the largest increase in terrorist deaths ever recorded by any country, increasing by over 300 percent to 7,512 fatalities." IEP also reported that Boko Haram was responsible for 10 of the 20 most fatal terrorist attacks worldwide in 2014.[6]

Boko Haram Today

Since that report was released, a multinational offensive against Boko Haram killed hundreds of militants and severely degraded the group's territorial control and capacity to confront national security forces directly (more below). This is the second retreat for the group since 2009, and demonstrates its comparative weakness when confronted with a well-organized and determined military force.

In an insurgency, however, the offense often has the advantage. Battered but undeterred, Boko Haram has turned again to asymmetric tactics on a rich array of targets. Relying primarily on suicide bombings, the group terrorizes public spaces that are notoriously difficult to secure, such as markets and transit depots. Attacks often feature multiple coordinated bombings[7] and increasingly rely on kidnapped women and girls.[8] These strikes have succeeded in re-establishing the group's pre-2015 daily tempo of causalities, killing and injuring upwards of 50-100 people in an average attack. While aiming at poorly defended rural areas and camps for the displaced, the group has also renewed its assault on the city of Maiduguri, now home to some two million people in a combination of permanent residents and refugees from the years of fighting in the region. This mix of attacks on urban and rural areas gives the population a sense that there is no refuge from Boko Haram's reign of terror.

Despite their continued ability to menace daily life in the northeast, just how large and capable the group is today compared to late 2014 is difficult to assess. Boko Haram's members seem to be scattered throughout the Nigerian countryside and the border regions with Chad, Niger, and

[3] Department of State, Nigeria Country Report on Human Rights, 2014.
[4] Laura Grossman, "Boko Haram's New Caliphate." *The Long War Journal*, August 25, 2015. http://www.longwarjournal.org/archives/2014/08/boko_harams_new_cali.php
[5] U.S. Department of State, Nigeria Country Report on Human Rights, 2014. http://www.state.gov/documents/organization/236604.pdf
[6] Institute for Economics and Peace, "Global Terrorism Index 2015: Measuring and Understanding the Impact of Terrorism." November, 2015. http://economicsandpeace.org/wp-content/uploads/2015/11/2015-Global-Terrorism-Index-Report.pdf
[7] "Nigeria Suicide Bombings Kill at Least 16 in Chibok." *The Guardian*, January 28, 2016
[8] "Teenager Seized for Boko Haram Attack Tells How She Tore off Suicide Vest and Fled." *The Guardian*, February 11, 2016

Cameroon. While there were reports that militants abandoned large weapons caches and vehicle depots when fleeing from government troops, they nevertheless have been using rocket-propelled grenades (RPGs) and small arms alongside their IEDs.[9] Their use of kidnapped women to execute suicide attacks, while tactically advantageous (providing greater access even to secured areas), also suggests a shrunken supply of adult male foot soldiers. The group has been reduced to ambushes along rural roads in lieu of territorial control. Shekau, too, has lowered his public profile, perhaps as a result of being subordinated to a region-wide Islamic State hierarchy.[10] Regardless, Boko Haram has retained a presence in and around the northeast, and continues to menace cities as far west as Kano and Zaria and as far south as Abuja. In short, Boko Haram has been set back on its heels, but this status may be temporary, and the group is by no means yet defeated.

A Networked Threat

Boko Haram has demonstrated its ambitions to join global Islamist terrorist movements since at least 2009. Shekau began by emulating al Qaeda propaganda and making efforts to connect with its core leadership. More recently, he signaled an affinity for the Islamic State. Not only did he begin to refer to the territory seized in northern Nigeria as a caliphate and express support for Abu Bakr al-Baghdadi, but Boko Haram also adopted the Islamic State's signature black flag.[11] By March of last year, Shekau publicly declared Boko Haram's allegiance to the organization, a fealty that al-Baghdadi eventually accepted.[12] Now, Boko Haram is attempting to re-brand itself as the Islamic State's "West Africa Province."

Despite the appearance of preferential alliances, growing links between al Qaeda-affiliated groups and the new allies of the Islamic State in Africa suggest there is more collaboration than rivalry among the continent's terrorist groups. They also suggest an increasing appreciation among these groups for a common purpose: the rejection of decades of failed governance in their home countries and an effort to replace those failures with a rigid form of Islamist authority.[13]

In fact, Boko Haram's connections with other African terrorist groups seem to have had a more tangible effect on their capacity to wage successful terrorist attacks than their communications with groups outside the continent. As early as 2010, the leader of al Qaeda in the Islamic Maghreb (AQIM), mainly operating out of northern Mali, expressed support for the group, while Boko Haram itself claimed in 2011 to have made contact with al Shabaab in Somalia. In 2012, Boko Haram reportedly sent dozens of operatives to AQIM-controlled areas in Mali to receive training, and those same operatives later returned to Nigeria with more sophisticated equipment, including shoulder-fired rockets.[14] AQIM, notorious kidnappers, may also have inspired Boko Haram to undertake kidnapping

---

[9] "Boko Haram Assault on Maiduguri Leaves Scores Dead in Nigeria." *Associated Press*, 28 December, 2015

[10] Jacob Zenn, "A Biography of Boko Haram and the Bay'a to al-Baghdadi." *CTC Sentinel*, Volume 8, Issue 3. Combatting Terrorism Center, West Point: March 2015. There are also claims that Shekau has been severely wounded or even killed, although audio and video of the putative leader keep surfacing, and there is no hard evidence of his demise. See Will Hartley, "On the ropes? Boko Haram attacks continue apace despite Nigerian claims." *Jane's Terrorism and Security Monitor*, October 1, 2015

[11] Pham, 2016, p. 23

[12] Zenn, 2015.

[13] For a further exploration of this phenomena, see Yaroslav Trofimov, "Jihad Comes to Africa." *Wall Street Journal*, February 5, 2016.

[14] Pham, 2016, p. 21

for ransom operations in earnest. Today, links between groups in Libya, Mali, Niger, and Nigeria are fluid and pragmatic. While different organizations still operate independently from each other and continue to focus on local objectives, the mentoring and mutual support available among terrorist groups fuel the radical Islamist momentum in West Africa.

Efforts to Counter Boko Haram

The Nigerian Response

As discussed above, the initial government response to Boko Haram was swift and brutally executed, imposing a series of setbacks on the organization. But under the leadership of Shekau, the insurgency regrouped and pushed back with increasingly lethality, leveraging their reconstituted numbers, training, and often-superior equipment. In this second phase of the group's development, Boko Haram's boldness and tactical dominance throughout began to push government forces out of much of the northeast. Declaring a state of emergency in the northern states of Borno, Adamawa, and Yobe, the Nigerian government launched a Joint Military Task Force (JTF) and tasked the 7th Infantry Division with pushing back against the group. Security forces reportedly responded to Boko Haram's brutality with their own, using ruthless tactics and indiscriminate violence to intimidate both the terrorists and any possible sympathizers.[15] In its 2014 Country Report on Human Rights, the State Department noted, "observers asserted that the climate of impunity for serious crimes led to the victimization of the civilian population by both Boko Haram and government forces."[16] Despite international pressure and a renewed effort to professionalize the military forces, accusations of extrajudicial killings continue to dog Nigerian forces today.[17]

Upon his election in 2015, Nigeria's new president, Muhammadu Buhari, himself a retired Major General in the Nigerian Army, pledged to defeat Boko Haram by the end of the year and took several actions to advance toward this goal, including moving the force headquarters from Abuja to Maiduguri and dismissing several senior military officers suspected of corruption. The government ostensibly has also increased resources for the military after years of under-investment, to include ensuring on-time personnel payment.[18] The reinvigorated effort, coupled with regional pressure on the group, is paying operational dividends, as Nigerian forces have successfully routed Boko Haram from all of the territory it previously held and seized weapons caches and destroyed former hideouts. At the same time, the Buhari administration has announced renewed efforts to investigate and prosecute military violations of human rights and corruption.[19] It is unclear how far these anti-corruption efforts aimed at the security services will truly go, but Buhari's efforts to date represent long-overdue steps in the right direction.

---

[15] Amnesty International, "Stars on their Shoulders, Blood on their Hands: War Crimes Committed by the Nigerian Military." June 2, 2015. https://www.amnesty.org/en/documents/afr44/1657/2015/en/

[16] U.S. Department of State, Nigeria Country Report on Human Rights, 2014.

[17] Michelle Faul and Ibrahim Abdulaziz, "Nigeria: People Detained by Military Disappear in Northeast." *The Washington Post*, February 20, 2016.

[18] Government of Nigeria Ministry of Budget and National Planning, "Appropriation Bill 2016." http://www.budgetoffice.gov.ng/pdfs/2016/2016AppropriationBill.pdf. See also, Muhammadu Buhari, "The Budget of Change." Speech Delivered to the National Assembly, December 22, 2015. http://www.budgetoffice.gov.ng/pdfs/2016/2016BudgetSpeech.pdf

[19] "Top Nigerian Military Officer Arrested Over Arms Scandal." *News24*, February 10, 2016. http://www.news24.com/Africa/News/top-nigerian-military-officer-arrested-over-arms-scandal-20160210-2

Regional Cooperation

Nigeria's revitalization of its counterterrorism operations was preceded by a regional and international push for collaboration to combat the threat in the wake of the Chibok kidnappings in 2014. Benin, Chad, Cameroon, Niger and Nigeria first met in Paris in May of 2014 along with representatives of the US, UK and EU to reactivate a long-standing but disused Multi-National Joint Task Force (MNJTF) originally organized through the Lake Chad Basin Commission. At a series of follow-on meetings, member countries pledged troops to the fight against Boko Haram, and by January of 2015 the African Union had endorsed plans for an 8,700-strong force and requested a UN trust fund to resource the effort. The MNJTF's tasks were to include targeted operations against Boko Haram, capturing members of the terrorist group, border security, recovery of abductees, regional coordination, and intelligence sharing.[20] Coupled with Nigeria's renewed offensive late in former President Goodluck Jonathan's term, regional efforts have seen tangible results. As recently as this month, Cameroon launched highly effective operations against Boko Haram both on its own soil and across the border into Nigeria.[21] There are also ongoing reports of Nigerian military operations destroying abandoned Boko Haram camps and hideouts.[22]

Unfortunately, the MNJTF has had an uneven start, with troop shortfalls and limited coordination efforts leading to questions about the task force's sustainability. Task force members focus largely on their own border regions, and it is unclear how much tactical, operational, or strategic coordination actually occurs.[23] Boko Haram also refused to go quietly, demonstrating its withering, if episodic, ability to overtake military bases. The capture of the town of Baga and the MNJTF headquarters there in early 2015 was an early setback for regional efforts.[24] Nevertheless, real operational gains have resulted from the combined, if not entirely coordinated, efforts.

Implications for Regional and International Security

It is too soon to tell how much of a practical impact on Boko Haram's operational capacity the contradictory forces of the regional offensive and the group's allegiance with the Islamic state will have. Military operations against the organization have certainly forced it to retreat from its long-held territory and hideouts, including in the Sambisa Forest. Meanwhile, there is some evidence that the Islamic State may be supporting improvements to Boko Haram's media campaign, but there are fewer signs of financial support or capacity building flowing to the West African affiliate. Some analysts speculate that the alliance largely served propaganda purposes for both groups, making the Islamic State look like it was expanding even under intense pressure in the Middle East and making Boko Haram look relevant to the global Islamist terrorist network.[25]

---

[20] Ionel Zamfield, "At a Glance: African-Led Counterterrorism Measures Against Boko Haram." European Parliamentary Research Service, March 2015. See also: Department of State 2014 Counterterrorism Report http://www.europarl.europa.eu/RegData/etudes/ATAG/2015/551302/EPRS_ATA(2015)551302_EN.pdf

[21] "Cameroon stages major attack on Boko Haram base in Nigeria." *Yahoo News/AFP*, Feb 16, 2016

[22] "Troops destroy Boko Haram camps in Sambisa, Alagarno." Vanguard News. February 17, 2016 http://www.vanguardngr.com/2016/02/troops-destroy-boko-haram-camps-in-sambisa-alagarno/

[23] Thomas Fessy, "Boko Haram: Can Regional Force Beat Nigeria's Militant Islamists?" *BBC News*, March 3, 2015. http://www.bbc.com/news/world-africa-31695508

[24] "The Massacre Nigeria Forgot: A Year after Boko Haram's Attack on Baga." *The Guardian*, 9 January, 2016. See also: Pham, 2016, p. 23

[25] "OSINT Summary: The Islamic State Accepts Boko Haram's Pledge of Allegiance." *Jane's Terrorism and Security Monitor*, April 1, 2015.

Nevertheless, a heightened and more sophisticated media profile may help attract regional fighters to Boko Haram from both West and North Africa, particularly if the group is able to reestablish safe havens inside Nigeria. Alternatively, if Nigerian security forces are able to hold territory recently re-won in the 2015 offensive, it is possible that Boko Haram operatives will scatter further afield to join more promising campaigns, in Mali, Libya, or elsewhere. There are also concerns that the regionalization of the response to Boko Haram through the MNJTF will lead to an expansion (or diffusion) of the group's military operations to Nigeria's neighbors. Already a presence in Cameroon and long responsible for kidnappings and raids there, Boko Haram has now threatened increased violence against targets in Chad and Niger in response to their involvement in the regional offensive.[26]

Beyond the continuing threat of attacks, the conflict has displaced upwards of two million people, many of whom are children under the age of five.[27] Such a large population of essentially migratory communities is having an enormous impact on the region's economy, society, and environment. Farms lie fallow and livelihoods have been abandoned. The region's cities, already suffering from inadequate infrastructure and water shortages, are now overtaxed by swelling populations as people seek refuge away from rural areas.

There is little evidence that Boko Haram, as an organization, has developed the capability to reach beyond West Africa, and it appears from the pattern of ongoing attacks that its sights are still set mainly on Nigerian targets. However, a sure sign of both the group's reach and the impact of its affiliation with the Islamic State would be any evidence that Boko Haram members were traveling to North Africa to participate in the wider IS fight. If Nigeria and its neighbors successfully maintain pressure on the group regionally, the international community would be wise to look for signs that Boko Haram fighters were migrating to other parts of Africa or offering their services to the Islamic State elsewhere.

What Partners Can Do

The brazenness of Boko Haram's ongoing attacks, especially against displaced civilians using kidnapped girls as suicide bombers, underscores the ongoing challenge that security forces face in defending northeastern communities. As it stands today, Boko Haram would likely attempt to recapture territory in the event of a weakening or withdrawal of government forces. Security must also be implemented in an environment with devastated infrastructure using police and military forces that will need to recover from years of under-investment and a severe trust gap with the local population. At the same time, the glut of refugees and the challenges behind reintegrating former Boko Haram captives indicate a humanitarian and social crisis that may long outlast the fighting.[28]

In such an environment, the Nigerian government must take a strong lead in developing the political will and financial commitment to provide holistic security in areas ravaged by Boko Haram. Such a

---

[26] Marc-Antoine Perouse de Montclos, "Boko Haram: Regional Issues Around the Uprising," Jean-Jaures Foundation, February 10, 2015. http://www.jean-jaures.org/Publications/Notes/Boko-Haram

[27] See UNICEF Nigeria plan for 2016: http://www.unicef.org/appeals/nigeria.html

[28] One acute example of this social stress is the plight of women and girls kidnapped by Boko Haram and the tenuous status of the children they have had a result of sexual abuse. See: International Alert and UNICEF, "Bad Blood: Perceptions of Children Born of Conflict-Related Sexual Violence and Women and Girls Associated with Boko Haram in Northeast Nigeria," February, 2016

security plan should include an effective policing capacity to protect the population and deny Boko Haram successful attacks, coupled with military operations when necessary. Both forces should be bolstered by intelligence capabilities and linked to an efficient justice sector able to conduct detention operations and swift prosecutions according to international standards for the just rule of law. All of this must be coupled with a robust development program that can provide basic services and infrastructure to long-neglected communities. Such an effort would be unprecedented in the north and take substantial political capital from Abuja and its international backers.

Partners can reinforce Nigerian-led efforts with continued diplomatic engagement, technical advising and support, equipment assistance, and expertise. The U.S., U.K., and the EU in particular have been continually involved in efforts to fill technical gaps. The UK announced at the end of December last year that it would increase its training and advisory force in Nigeria to 300 personnel.[29] Meanwhile, the EU has dedicated tens of millions of Euros to providing humanitarian assistance to Boko Haram's victims.[30] After the 2014 Chibok kidnapping, the U.S. and Nigeria renewed efforts at counter-Boko Haram collaboration, with the U.S. deploying an interagency advisory team to Abuja. More recently, the Defense Department deployed 300 forces to Cameroon to support intelligence, surveillance, and reconnaissance operations focused on Boko Haram.[31] Nigeria is also a beneficiary of multiple U.S. security assistance programs, including the new Security Governance Initiative, the Global Security Contingency Fund, and the Counterterrorism Partnership Fund. Through these programs the U.S. has recently provided communications gear and equipment to Nigeria, including a recent delivery of 24 mine-resistant, ambush protected vehicles (MRAPs). The U.S. also supports efforts by other regional partners to combat Boko Haram, including Niger and Cameroon,[32] and frequently consults with European partners to coordinate efforts and share information. This broad approach ensures that the counter-Boko Haram effort is a diversified and sustainable portfolio of investment in regional partners.

Conclusion

International efforts can only proceed at the pace set by Nigeria. The U.S. recently re-started infantry battalion training after a long hiatus,[33] with plans to build on such engagements and ongoing evaluations of Nigerian equipment requests. Continued accusations of human rights violations by Nigerian security forces and Nigeria's own concerns about protecting its sovereignty mean that all external support is preceded with careful and mutual evaluations of both sides' intentions. These engagements are complex but must continue in order to sustain pressure on Boko Haram. The U.S. and other Nigerian partners should continue to point out the connections between government conduct in the north and the resilience and support of local communities, sustaining an upper hand against Boko Haram.

Boko Haram has shown its own resilience over almost 14 years of organizational contraction and expansion. All told, the conflict has resulted in the deaths of some 20,000 people and displaced

[29] "UK to Send More Armed Forces to Nigeria to Advise on Boko Haram." *The Guardian*, 21 December, 2015.
[30] European Commission, Press Release, "EU Boosts Humanitarian Aid to Those Displaced by Boko Haram Violence." June 18, 2015. http://europa.eu/rapid/press-release_IP-15-5213_en.htm
[31] White House, "Letter from the President—War Powers Resolution Regarding Cameroon." October 14, 2015. https://www.whitehouse.gov/the-press-office/2015/10/14/letter-from-president-war-powers-resolution-cameroon
[32] "US Gives Nigeria 24 Armored Vehicles for Boko Haram Fight." *Asia News Monitor*, January 11, 2016
[33] Helene Cooper, "Rifts between U.S. and Nigeria Impeding Fight Against Boko Haram." *The New York Times*, January 24, 2015.

approximately 2 million,[34] and the group's unabated bombing campaign belies premature claims about its operational defeat. And its ability to generate an endorsement from the Islamic State, while not necessarily a sign of operational strength, demonstrates the group's ability to adapt and leverage relationships in order to survive. The Nigerian government must capitalize on recent operational successes in the north to build a lasting edifice against terrorist violence, and its international partners must remain vigilant against the group's revival and possible encroachment abroad.

---

[34] Council on Foreign Relations, "Nigeria Security Tracker." http://www.cfr.org/nigeria/nigeria-security-tracker/p29483

Mr. POE. Thank you very much.

Dr. Gartenstein-Ross, it is your turn.

STATEMENT OF DAVEED GARTENSTEIN–ROSS, PH.D., SENIOR FELLOW, FOUNDATION FOR DEFENSE OF DEMOCRACIES

Mr. GARTENSTEIN-ROSS. Thank you, Chairman Poe, Ranking Member Keating, and distinguished members. As Chairman Poe mentioned, I was a last-minute addition to this panel, substituting in for Jacob Zenn whose written statement, I think, is very granular, and I very much recommend.

I think the previous two statements do a very good job of providing, in detail, the situation on the ground, so what I want to do is take a somewhat broader look at the question of where is Boko Haram today compared to where it was in the past, and what do we need to do to more effectively address not just Boko Haram but the challenge of other militant groups as well?

Ms. Friend referred to previous Boko Haram retreats. You can tabulate them in different ways. I count personally at least two since 2009. One of them in '09 is when Boko Haram was essentially defeated. Its leader Mohammed Yusuf was killed, and around 1,000 members were killed during that period. It was scattered and relied upon primarily al-Qaeda and the Islamic Maghreb, but also al-Shabaab in Somalia to help it regenerate. In 2013, the Nigerian Government launched an offensive starting in May against Boko Haram which also pushed it back, though not as significantly.

I think that, right now, Boko Haram is more vulnerable than what it was in 2013. President Buhari has more of a political incentive to maintain the Boko Haram than there was back in 2013. You have multiple states' militaries going after the militant group.

And a third thing is we have talked about the defection to the Islamic State. Now there is problems with the defection from our perspective, but also there is some opportunity. I think it makes them more vulnerable, because previously Boko Haram, when it was part of the al-Qaeda network, its major source of strength outside of Nigeria was in Mali. Today its major source of strength is in Libya which is further away. It was much easier for them to use surrounding territories when they were part of the al-Qaeda network.

But the question really is, how effectively will we take advantage of this opening of these vulnerabilities and craft a solution? One sad conclusion that I have reached is that we as a government are just not very good at fighting against violent non-state actors. If you look at our record over the past decade and a half when this was a top strategic priority, we have not been effective. In the 21st century you have perhaps only two major violent non-state actor groups who have been defeated. One of them, the LTTE in Sri Lanka which was wiped out by the Sri Lankan Government, and the other one being the Islamic Movement of Uzbekistan which was wiped out by the Taliban in recent months. Overall, we have trouble.

So what I would point to as some of the source of our trouble is that violent non-state actors are very much, they are very old in conception, but in other ways they are a 21st century problem. If you look at the 20th century, it is what I call the Westphalian moment when the state system inscribed in the Peace of Westphalia was so dominant that non-state actors who were launching insurgencies or who were nationalist terrorist groups couldn't think of any other way to be. They wanted to be states, ranging from the anti-Colonial insurgencies to terrorist groups like the IRA, the LTTE, Palestinian terrorist groups, the ETA, all of these wanted to be states. In the 21st century you are seeing groups like ISIS, Boko, al-Qaeda, which are able to do many things states do—provide services, govern. They don't want to have any part of the state system.

I would analogize this to what we are seeing in the economics sphere because it is a very similar situation. In the economic sphere, going to the very end of the 20th century, conventional wisdom was that bigger was better; that when Blockbuster came into town it was going to drive your local video store out; that bookstores like Borders would be able to, with their megastores, dominate local markets. But these businesses failed to adapt to changing circumstances. They were too bureaucratic, too slow to adjust strategically. Borders didn't even have a Web site until 1998, 3 years after Amazon launched. When it finally put together its own e-reader to compete with Kindle, they made people come into the store to actually go to a download station which defeated the purpose of online shopping.

That is what our Government is. We are very slow to adapt. Violent non-state actors are like start-ups in the political organizing sphere. They have the same advantages. They are able to adapt strategically, quickly, they don't face our bureaucracy, and part of the move of ISIS into Africa, part of that story is ISIS actually convincing the media that they controlled a city in Libya that they didn't, the city of Derna.

They control Sirte today, but at the time that BBC, CNN and others reported on ISIS' control of Derna, which helped show Boko how strong ISIS was, they did not control Derna. And one thing that was frustrating for me in talking to multiple people within the U.S. Government was that there was no one in place to puncture this myth, and it was bad for us. It was bad for us that they were able to sustain this myth.

So looking at, I would say part of what we should be talking about, we should be talking about the policy solutions put forward here because these are very good, and as was said by Ms. Cooke, there is a sense of urgency. We need to act. But at the same time we have to think about our organizational structure, because many of the problems that we confront systemically in this area come down to lack of coordination, inefficient contracting rules, and not having the right people in place for this.

We need to, just like big industries have adapted by understanding the principles of their competitors we need to do the same thing, because we have an organizational structure that is not well suited for 21st century challenges. Thank you.

[Mr. Gartenstein-Ross did not submit a prepared statement.]

Mr. POE. I thank all of our witnesses. I recognize myself for 5 minutes of questions. Boko Haram was established in 2002. We had a hearing in 2013 wanting to know why they weren't part of the Foreign Terrorist Organization. The day before the hearing, ironically, the State Department designated them as a Foreign Terrorist Organization. That brings with it certain status that we supposedly as a nation focus on that organization because they are a Foreign Terrorist Organization.

My question to you, has anything happened to Boko Haram because they are now a Foreign Terrorist Organization? Have we imposed any of the things we can do such as sanctions and going after the finances against Boko Haram since that? Any of you want to weigh in on that? Ms. Cooke?

Ms. COOKE. Sure. I think because of the nature of Boko Haram at that time and the fact that it doesn't bank in the United States, its members don't travel to the United States, it doesn't bank through formal institutions, I think some of the tools of the Foreign Terrorist Organization declaration weren't particularly helpful and didn't add a great deal except perhaps drawing greater U.S. policymaker attention to the group.

I think now, now that the Nigerian Government itself has made cutting the group's financial sources a priority and President Buhari mentioned that in his inaugural address and we know that the group has expanded its regional connections, I think this is a moment where we can bring those tools much more into play to assist the Nigerians in doing that. That has to be done in coordination with other international and regional law enforcement agencies and financial institutions. That is a vital priority in preventing their eventual regeneration.

Mr. POE. The Boko Haram has a reputation, and I think it is based on facts, unfortunately, of targeting young women, Christian women, and either forcing them to convert or pay the consequences of sex slavery or murder. Is this a fundamental principle of this specific terrorist organization? Dr. Ross, do you want to weigh in on that?

Mr. GARTENSTEIN-ROSS. It is a fundamental principle of a number of different jihadist organizations. It is a fundamental principle of Boko Haram. ISIS also has done the same thing if you look at their treatment of Yazidis. And if you look at the Nusra Front, which is al-Qaeda's affiliate in Syria, they also have a forced conversion program that they have imposed upon the Druze sect, which I read about in Foreign Affairs last year. So the answer is an unequivocal yes.

Mr. POE. The activity of murdering folks, young females, Christians, would that in your opinion, any of you, fit the definition of genocide? Ms. Cooke, yes or no?

Ms. COOKE. Well, I think they are less, they are indiscriminate in their attacks and we have to acknowledge that many, many of their victims, and perhaps the majority, have been Muslims who equally are forced to adapt this much, this very foreign version of Islam. So I don't know that that label applies in this case.

Mr. POE. Okay. Anybody else?

Mr. GARTENSTEIN-ROSS. I believe it applies, and much more so in Iraq and Syria where you actually have governance. Boko Haram's most recent experience with governance in Borno was very short-lived, so you didn't get to see the program get borne out. But the definition of genocide is intent to destroy in whole or in part. And that is absolutely what ISIS did to the Yazidis. It is absolutely what right now Nusra is doing to the Druze. And it, in my view, absolutely applies to what is being done to the Christians as well.

You can see ISIS' cancellation of the jizya, which is the tax that non-Muslims who are concerned People of the Book can pay to continue practicing their religion, they cancelled the jizya in Mosul thus causing all Christians to flee the city. In my view it is actually unequivocal.

It is absolutely correct what Ms. Cooke said that they do also target Muslims, but the intent to destroy in my view is very clear. They are going to try to subjugate Muslims, but groups that are not like them with a few minor exceptions including Shia Muslims are groups that they are absolutely out to destroy.

Mr. POE. Last question. Ms. Friend, you haven't answered any of my questions, or I haven't asked you any, but the world heard about those girls that were kidnapped and you mentioned in your testimony we don't really know what happened to them. What happened to them? What do you think happened to them, those 200 to 300 girls?

Ms. FRIEND. Well, sir, I can only speculate what happened to them. And my personal speculation is that some of them were sold into human trafficking, some of them were taken on as child brides or sex slaves, and I fear that some of them have been used in these suicide bombings that we are now hearing about. Boko Haram has kidnapped so many children and so many people over time that it is very hard to sort out especially in suicide bombings who is who, but that is my fear and what makes logical sense to me.

But it is true that, as far as we know, as far as the Nigerians know, members of the Joint Task Force that most of those girls are still unaccounted for. I believe something like 57 escaped at the time, so we are looking at closer to 200 girls that are still missing. But President Buhari recently also sounded a note of caution about being able to recover them. So even Buhari who is quite optimistic about defeat of the Boko Haram is not optimistic about recovery of the girls at this point unfortunately.

Mr. POE. All right, thank you very much. My time is expired and I will yield to the gentleman from Massachusetts for his questions.

Mr. KEATING. Thank you, Mr. Chairman. Since Boko Haram's pledge of allegiance to ISIL, has that had an effect on its recruitment and its retention capabilities? And also, where is it getting its financing? Where is it getting its weapons and supplies from specifically? You mentioned, I think, Ms. Friend, that some of it is selling, the human trafficking gain, financial gains from that. But what else, and where is it getting the weapons?

Ms. FRIEND. Yes, sir. As far as financing goes, Jennifer and I were talking about it a little bit before the hearing began. Traditionally they got much of their financing through extortion, through bank robberies, through looting. Jennifer has some more insights, I think, on sort of more recent information about where they might be getting more support. But those have been their traditional sources. A lot of the kinds of attacks that they undertake are not high cost. They use very low tech IEDs, for example, so unfortunately a little bit of money goes a long way for this group.

Mr. KEATING. A couple of, if I could, a couple of more recent developments in the last 2 or 3 months I just want to get your opinions on. Number one, in December the Nigerian military attacked and killed a number of Shia Muslims in the town of Zaria. And do you think that is an indication of future trends for sectarian violence, and what is the government doing to try and quell the Sunni-Shia tensions?

Ms. COOKE. I think it is a very good question and there is still a lot that is not known about the circumstances of the Zaria attack that killed some 400 Shiite Muslims and grievously wounded the group's leader Zakzaky. There is an investigation underway and that may give more clarity. Senior officials that I have spoken to hint at some kind of imminent and dangerous threat, but there is not a lot of public discourse on that.

Mr. KEATING. The other thing that I just want to touch upon, the last couple of months there have been reports through separate media sources about Cameroonians committing human rights abuses inside Nigeria. Do you have any comments on that and what the effect could be and how legitimate those reports are?

Ms. COOKE. I haven't heard those reports. But in terms of the Shiite split, I think that the Nigerian Government needs to tread very carefully there. Iran called, President Rouhani called President Buhari shortly thereafter. The Saudi Arabian king called him shortly thereafter. What you don't want to see is some ideological proxy playing out in the north of Nigeria.

Mr. KEATING. That is my fear as well. Ms. Friend?

Ms. FRIEND. Sir, if I may add, Nigeria also has had years and years of Christian-Muslim violence that is a major problem for stability in the country. Going further into sectarian violence amongst Muslims plays exactly into Boko Haram's hands.

And so I completely agree with Jennifer on this case. I think the government has to be very careful about this and not improve the narrative for Boko Haram while they are at it.

Mr. KEATING. Another concern I had just recently is just what is occurring in terms of the shift, if there is a shift at all, with President Goodluck Jonathan using private forces, mercenaries as well? The President, Buhari, rather, he wanted to shift away from that. Is that happening, or is there still use of mercenaries at all, and are there difficulties because of the use of those mercenaries and having control over them and their conduct as well?

Ms. COOKE. I am one of the people that think, actually, the South African contractors actually contributed a good deal to better tactics and more sustained and coordinated attacks to push Boko Haram out of the territories.

Mr. KEATING. Are they still using those forces?

Ms. COOKE. They are not still using them and they may recur. There may be private contractors brought on again, whether it is these same or not. So that is at an end right now. That was at a time that the United States, for example, did not want to provide certain materiel to the Nigerian Government because of human rights abuses.

Mr. KEATING. Well, just quickly, listening to all of your testimony, I don't think there is a conflict but it is worth commenting on. Ms. Cooke, you mentioned that some of the gains we made were with media, and part of that might be quelling their ability to do it, but Dr. Gartenstein-Ross mentioned our inability to deal with these issues of propaganda or media as well. Is there a way to reconcile those two things if indeed there is a conflict in your two statements?

Ms. COOKE. Well, we believe that Abubakar Shekau has been taken out and he was—whether 2 years ago followed by imposters or just recently—and he was really the center of the media propaganda effort. He has not been seen on the scene since March. But regeneration will certainly entail a renewal of more nimble sophisticated media techniques.

Mr. KEATING. And do you agree with Dr. Gartenstein-Ross that we have to do a better job of sort of puncturing the myths that are out there?

Ms. COOKE. Absolutely. We are slower on that online stuff than these young militants.

Mr. KEATING. My time is expired. I yield back, Mr. Chairman.

Mr. POE. I thank the gentleman from Massachusetts.

Mr. Perry?

Mr. PERRY. Thank you, Mr. Chairman. Ms. Cooke, in your opinion, why did it take us so long to designate Boko Haram a terrorist organization?

Ms. COOKE. Well, and I testified before this hearing some time back shortly after Boko Haram reemerged after 2009. At that time the group was extremely fractured. We didn't really have a sense of what was Boko Haram. Nigeria at that time did not want it designated an FTO organization, in part because there were certain elements within it that it felt that it could peel away, and the potential of having talks with certain elements within Boko Haram was very popular in Nigeria, across Nigeria.

To my mind, at that time the designation didn't give you tools that would make, be more effective. As I said, they don't bank in the United States, they don't use banking institutions. But what it might have done at that time was give greater coherence to a group that was very fractured and ideologically and internally divided at that time.

I think the eventual call was right. But at that time I think there is a legitimate difference of opinion on whether it should have happened or not. My sense was that, because the Nigerian Government didn't want it, because it might have lent that greater coherence and brand name to the group, we should have postponed it.

Mr. PERRY. I guess I understand. It is in their country and they had reservations about it, but in hindsight.

Ms. COOKE. Well, there is no question——

Mr. PERRY. I mean, you are never going to know, right? You are never going to know if we would have designated it earlier whether it would have, would it be the advent of the coalescing of those desperate portions.

Ms. COOKE. That is right. But we don't know that it would have added any benefit in our fight against Boko Haram since the tool is directed at bank accounts, asset freezes, sanctions and so forth.

Mr. PERRY. And that is the only thing as you understand it in designating——

Ms. COOKE. Well, I know, but it elevates attention to the group at that time.

Mr. PERRY. Right.

Ms. COOKE. As I said, I think there are legitimate differences of opinion. There was a trade-off. There was a chance at that time of dividing the group. And eventually as we know the designation was given.

Mr. PERRY. So what is the trigger? So we are watching it. The government, the local government, state government doesn't want them to be designated for whatever they see as legitimate reasons. We don't want to increase the visibility and have these desperate organizations coalesce, but at what point do we say enough is enough? The ends would be that we don't want them to be, these groups to become as powerful as this one has become and pervasive as it has, so what is the trigger point? What do we get out of this model for the next model?

Ms. COOKE. Well, look, I think in every instance there is going to be a debate within the administration with the Congress on what makes most sense in that particular very unique context. And I don't think there is going to be, there is no set trigger point in anything. I think you have to look at the totality of the benefits and the potential costs.

Mr. PERRY. So fair enough. Which organizations have we not designated or that we have designated a terrorist organization that has caused the coalescing? Is there any empirical data? Is there anything to say that—these are going to keep springing up, right? If it is not here, it is going to be somewhere.

Ms. COOKE. Well, some people thought that the designation of Shabaab kind of came at a poor moment, for example, and kind of elevated, gave them a propaganda tool. And as I said, I think in retrospect the FTO designation didn't fundamentally change how we were dealing with Boko Haram at the time.

Mr. PERRY. So do we need to change what the FTO designation means in real terms, what that construct is? Is it just banking or is it something—do we need take a look at that looking at—you were talking about earlier about how our Government—or maybe it was you, Dr. Ross, about how we are slow to react because of a bureaucracy and so on and so forth, and they are very quick to react. So is there something that we need to take a look at it in this paradigm that needs to change so that our reaction is meaningful in thwarting these organizations?

Ms. COOKE. Well, I would have to reflect a little bit on what that might be. I think recognizing the danger and the potential of the group is important, and if the FTO designation does that that is a loss in retrospect.

Mr. PERRY. But how many do we know that we haven't designated that since we didn't designate them they kind of fizzled out on their own? What does that look like? What is that——

Ms. COOKE. Well, I don't know the record of debates on the FTO designation.

Mr. PERRY. No, no. I am not talking about the record of the debates. I am talking about which organizations where we are saying, well, we are thinking about designating them in an FTO, but if we do it might heighten awareness to them and actually make them what they are aspiring to be, so let us hold off. How many of those are out there that we know of where we were successful by not designating them and then they fizzled out? Do we know what that number is?

Ms. COOKE. I don't.

Mr. PERRY. And I will tell you, with indulgence, Mr. Chairman, the context is, is that it seems to me we keep waiting for whatever reason, maybe legitimate and maybe not, to designate some of these people that go around doing the horrific things that they do, and my experience has been from at least watching from afar is that we wait too long, they metastasize, they become very powerful and then we have got to deal with this.

So if we are looking at this as a model for future operations and future decisions, it seems to me we ought to get something out of it, which is some kind of standard or trigger point or something, by which we say that is enough. We don't want it to get—we don't want to have this problem get any bigger than it is and then do something as opposed to, well, it is all episodic and today it is this one and tomorrow it is that one and we are just going to do it; we are going to wing it every time, because it seems to me we have been failing at winging it. That is my opinion.

With that, Mr. Chairman, I yield.

Mr. POE. I thank the gentleman. The chair recognizes the gentleman from New York, Mr. Higgins.

Mr. HIGGINS. Thank you, Mr. Chairman. Dr. Ross, you had indicated, you were talking about violent non-state actors before and you characterized Boko Haram as a violent non-state actor. Yet, they use brutal killings of innocent people as a method to demonstrate the incapacity of the Nigerian state. They terrorize local populations. They engage the military in bloody conflict. They seek to destabilize and overthrow the government and install an Islamic caliphate. So are they not, don't they have a state controlled aspiration?

Mr. GARTENSTEIN-ROSS. Absolutely they do. I use the term ''violent non-state actor'' because to me it is a catch-all term that could include different modes of military operation, right. We tend right now in discourse to refer to these groups as terrorist groups, which is accurate for most of them, but at the same time for Boko it is not just a terrorist group. Usually a terrorist group is relatively weak and can't militarily engage, can't hold territory. They use terrorism to try to provoke a state reaction and rally a community to their side.

Boko, in contrast, was last year at this time the dominant force in Borno State in northeastern Nigeria. So they also could engage in insurgent warfare, they are also able to seize territory and govern. That is why I use that particular term.

Mr. HIGGINS. Yes. Well, look at, I think on the whole of Africa as a continent it is 55 countries now including South Sudan, the newest country in the world. How many failed states are in the continent of Africa?

Mr. GARTENSTEIN-ROSS. Off the top of my head and the fact that it is hard to tabulate, but a very easy answer is there is much more than we should be comfortable with and there is also those states which aren't failed but are in danger of failing. Tunisia, for example, which nobody would call a failed state is fundamentally, existentially threatened by these attacks on its tourist industry which could send it into an economic death spiral.

Mr. HIGGINS. Boko Haram which literally is ''Western education is forbidden'' aligns itself with ISIS. ISIS seems to have maybe not shifted, but emphasized less emphasis on oil revenues, more on territorial gains, because the more territory they can control the more they can impose taxes, they can preside over countries and using that as leverage to extract money to support their bloody deeds all over.

Given the fragile state of affairs in Africa, particularly Central Africa, is Africa a means to provide for access to southern Europe?

Mr. GARTENSTEIN-ROSS. Yes. That shouldn't be overstated, but it certainly is something that has been discussed in ISIS propaganda. The degree to which Europe is able to control the flow in by sea is limited, and it seems that already terrorist groups to a limited extent are trying to place operatives amongst the refugee inflow.

Mr. HIGGINS. What is the role, if any, of the African Union?

Mr. GARTENSTEIN-ROSS. I believe the African Union is charged obviously with a number of things including security. I mean, I think when you are looking at Africa there is two different models, right.

Mr. HIGGINS. Security for whom?

Mr. GARTENSTEIN-ROSS. Well, security for African states. So I was——

Mr. HIGGINS. All right. What is the population of the continent with its 55 countries of Africa?

Mr. GARTENSTEIN-ROSS. Off the top of my head?

Ms. COOKE. Billion-plus.

Mr. HIGGINS. Billion-plus? Billion? How many African Union military personnel are engaged, activated?

Mr. GARTENSTEIN-ROSS. It is limited. I mean, you have——

Mr. HIGGINS. About?

Mr. GARTENSTEIN-ROSS. Well, in Somalia it is about today, I think, sort of reaching 9,000 and 12,000. Then you have the Ecowas and Minusma contingents in Mali. The number is in the tens of thousands as opposed to——

Mr. HIGGINS. Let me ask this. Let me put it to you another way. How many stable countries are there in Africa? One, two?

Ms. COOKE: Many. Many.

Mr. GARTENSTEIN-ROSS. Yes, 30, 40. The majority are stable. But I will say one thing to cap this, which is as you said, ISIS, its model right now is to seize territory and to hold territory. I mean, we have talked about al-Qaeda and how Boko went over from al-Qaeda to ISIS. To me, I am more worried about al-Qaeda's strategy which seems to be a strategy of progressive destabilization.

So if you look at Libya, for example, ISIS does hold territory. And one of the things that makes action, military action, against ISIS in Sirte, such a difficult thing for us to agree to is that if you were to push ISIS out, al-Qaeda could well be the beneficiary. So you retake a city from ISIS without actually winning anything for it.

I am much more concerned about this progressive destabilization. Right now you can see Boko tried to control Borno State. It got pushed out. Sometimes you can get too greedy. But one thing, given population pressures, resource pressures including pressures on the water supply in numerous countries, one thing that you can bet on in the longer term is it is hard to keep these countries stable. So if I am looking at it, it is hard to prevent actors like this whose long term goal is to destabilize and to capitalize off of that destabilization.

Mr. HIGGINS. Just a final thought, Mr. Chairman. Look at South Sudan. South Sudan became the newest country in the world in July 2011. And they were in a civil war with Sudan for 30 years, and they have become their own state and primarily Christian in the south, and now there is tribal battle between the Dinkas and the Nuers. And we just saw a Protection of Civilians facility attacked by government officials where some 20,000 people were essentially murdered and another 30,000 displaced, again, and you talk to officials in South Sudan who want to have diplomatic relations with us and they talk about how we have to get the U.N. out of there. Well, the only organization that is protecting people is the United Nations. It is the second largest mission in the world.

So these corrupt governments, and if you look at the World Economic Forum, and you see that they only contribute about 5 percent of their budgets and they are oil-rich. I mean, South Sudan, most of the oil reserves are in the south, but the infrastructure is in the north. They have the potential. But less than 5 percent goes to education, to health care, to infrastructure. I mean, you can't move around South Sudan but for about a 2-mile radius within the capital city of Juba. This is a major problem. And I don't have a solution, but it obviously appears as though whatever strategy is being deployed has been an abject failure. It is going to continue to fail and so long as there is failed states they are going to serve as a breeding ground for groups like this and ISIS.

Mr. GARTENSTEIN-ROSS. If I may, because I know that we are over time, I just want to refer back to what I said in my oral statement. That is why I think it is so important for us to think about our own internal structures for decision making, because what you are referring to—look, beating these groups militarily is in my view the easy part. The hard part is leaving behind something stable and pushing them back as part of a coordinated strategy.

And within government my view is that we are absolutely dysfunctional in this regard. Like, we have a lot of trouble leaving behind something that is stable and we need to think about why that is. And a lot of it maybe comes down to our organizational structure is just not suited for a lot of these tasks. I believe it can be, but this is absolutely a problem and one that we shouldn't push to the side when we are thinking about these regions and trying to think of what is a good policy. The fact that we have systemically been awful at executing, and leaving behind stability has to be a part of the discussion and something that we think about as we think about our own Government for the 21st century.

Mr. HIGGINS: Who is we?

Mr. GARTENSTEIN-ROSS. Well, we would be you all, policymakers who are in a very good position to hold hearings looking at this. Those of us who are outside of government working in the think tanks here and the like also are positioned to push the ball forward, but ultimately, to me the people who are in the best position to ask these questions and to get action on them are elected members of the legislature. To me that is really where the center is for the kind of governmental reforms we need. I think the White House as well.

Mr. POE. The gentleman's time has expired. I have been very liberal on this issue, a word I don't use very often. The chair will recognize the gentlelady from Florida, Ms. Wilson, who is not a member of this subcommittee but is invited to ask questions because this is an important issue for her. The chair recognizes Ms. Wilson from Florida.

Ms. WILSON. Thank you so much for having this hearing today. It is truly, truly needed. And I have several questions. I hope I don't run out of time.

But when President Buhari won the election in part because of his commitment to defeating Boko Haram, he contends that the group has been technically defeated. Is Boko Haram stronger or weaker since Buhari has taken over? That is number one.

And number two, because of Nigeria's human rights record—and we went to Nigeria twice and they were asking for the ability to buy arms and weapons from the United States and something called the Leahy Law prevents that. How do you get around the Leahy Law? How many people do you kill? Because Boko Haram according to all national newspapers is number one of the most terrorist, they have killed more people than any other terrorist group in the world. So when are we able to get the right people in the right places to defeat them? This is for anyone who can answer.

Ms. COOKE. I think, and as I said in my remarks, I think Boko Haram is very much weaker, but that does not mean that it is any less lethal and dangerous for the communities of that region, and we have seen that in the horrific attacks of the last few weeks. So this is a moment to weaken them even further and to eliminate their ability to then regenerate.

I think the asymmetrical attacks that they now launch that is a much more vexing problem because the area is so vast than just clearing them off of territory. And that requires very nimble responses, much better communication among military forces and with the communities and the capacity to move very quickly and respond.

On the Leahy Law, I fully support the principles and the logic behind the Leahy Law. I do think there might be, there should be room for some flexibility in looking at this so it is applied less broadly to entire units. Perhaps focus on individuals or smaller units. You look at——

Ms. WILSON. I don't want to cut you off, but that is the answer we got from, actually, the senator himself.

Ms. COOKE. And as I said, I think——

Ms. WILSON. That this was something. And then I want to ask this. We met with senators here from Nigeria, senators who represent different parts of Nigeria, and we met with them in Nigeria. And they say that they know where the girls are and there is—is this true? Is there any truth about President Buhari actively bartering with the appropriate leader of Boko Haram in exchange for the girls; that they are held captive in a secluded, secure area in the forest? Is there any truth to that?

Ms. COOKE. Well, there may be efforts to connect with the group to negotiate some release. No one of the thousands of members of Boko Haram that have been captured, of the thousands of women and girls that have been captured, no one has seen a Chibok girl. And that is just a remarkable mystery. I think many people I talk to think that they are broken into much smaller groups, married away, and possibly in the northern mountains of Cameroon, in Niger and elsewhere. This is just, it is a tragic mystery as to where they have gone. I am sure——

Ms. WILSON. Do you think if one of them, do you think that if they were, just one would appear, if they were married away, or someone out of all of those girls could have escaped, gotten back home or went and told someone that they were a Chibok girl, because that is all I am listening for.

Ms. COOKE. It has not happened.

Ms. WILSON. And I am looking for a mass grave to see where they all are, because this is——

Ms. COOKE. That has not been found, nor has any——

Ms. WILSON. That has not been found and they have not been found. So what do we do to sensitize the nation, sensitize America that this is an issue that is even threatening our homeland, because we don't know what Boko Haram has in mind, just like we don't know what ISIS has in mind with influencing African American boys in our inner cities.

And all of this Internet activity back and forth, and has anyone looked into that? And it is my understanding that there is a whole department at the State Department that deals with Boko Haram, and there are analysts there who just track Boko Haram. Are you aware of that?

Ms. COOKE. Well, I know that there is an interagency kind of co-operation group within the State Department and they have expanded their coordination and presence on Boko Haram. I don't know the number.

Ms. WILSON. What about the threat to the homeland, to our homeland from Boko Haram? Just like we are all afraid that ISIS is going to find its way in the United States, is anyone afraid that Boko Haram is going to find its way into our inner cities?

Ms. COOKE. I don't want to monopolize, but——

Ms. FRIEND. Ma'am, I don't——

Ms. WILSON. Has it been discussed at all in your think tanks?

Ms. FRIEND. I don't think there is a huge concern about that. There of course is, because of the nature of these groups where you can get one or two operatives through by hook or by crook, it is always a concern. But I think in a rack and stack of groups around the world there is less concern that Boko Haram poses an immediate direct threat to the U.S. homeland, and more concern about the threat they pose to Nigeria and the surrounding region. And also, of course, concern about this newfound connection with the Islamic State and what that really implies and entails.

One of the members earlier asked me, it was Mr. Higgins, asked about the threat to Europe. And of course our European allies are very concerned about a threat from ISIS coming especially out of

Libya, but North Africa in general. So those are the immediate threats. But of course from my time inside the executive branch, everyone is always on the lookout for the metastasization of such groups and for the evolving threat that Boko Haram could be posing to us, but at this time right now my understanding is it is less of a concern that they pose a direct threat to the homeland.

Ms. WILSON. When does it become an imminent threat, when it hits?

Ms. FRIEND. No, ma'am. I think when you start seeing, and of course this would be in a closed hearing and I don't have such information right now, but the kinds of things you would see would be direct communications between either foreign nationals in the United States or even American citizens with either facilitators that are talking to Boko Haram or with Boko Haram members themselves. I was never on the intel side so I am not as expert in that kind of thing, but when I saw finished intelligence that was the kinds of things that you look for.

Ms. WILSON. All right, Mr. Chair.

Mr. POE. I thank the gentlelady. I want to follow up on a question she had about what happened to the girls. Have any of them been ransomed back to their families?

Ms. COOKE. Not to my knowledge and not to the knowledge of the people I spoke to in Maiduguri and Abuja.

Mr. POE. And the other question she had was regarding mass graves of these girls. Has there been any evidence that they have all been killed or murdered somewhere? I mean, is there any evidence of that or is it just like you have mentioned, Ms. Friend, that they have gone different ways, all bad ways, but they have disappeared in different ways other than this murder?.

Ms. FRIEND. Yes, Mr. Chairman, my understanding from Amnesty International who I think has done the best work on looking for mass graves, mass graves have largely been found to have adult or teenage males in them. There was one that Amnesty identified outside the Giwa barracks, for example, that was largely males. Again my speculation is that young girls are financially valuable and so they would first try either to keep them themselves for domestic purposes or to sell them again into trafficking or slavery because they could make money that way. But again, that is my speculation. No one knows. It is truly a mystery.

Mr. POE. Thank you. The chair also has another Member of Congress here as a guest, Ms. Jackson Lee from Texas, and the chair will recognize her for her questions.

Ms. JACKSON LEE. Mr. Chairman and Ranking Member, let me thank you very much. And I am going to probably make comments because I think Mr. Gartenstein-Ross, your pointing back to policymakers and legislators are very important. There is a level of frustration and we have joined a lot of colleagues in our frustration for Boko Haram which is particularly a unique entity. I went to Boko Haram with a number of members and we have since gone back to Nigeria and Borno State, the first time, when the girls were first taken, trying to raise the ante and before the election of President Buhari and Goodluck Jonathan was in office.

So I just want—I think your title deals with the security issue, and I just want just a pointed yes or no of the capacity of the Nigerian forces to extinguish Boko Haram.

Mr. GARTENSTEIN-ROSS. I think their capacity is low. But I also want to point to the fact that you have multiple nations' militaries, of them I assess the Nigerians as being one of the less capable forces.

Ms. JACKSON LEE. That is unique, and I don't want to interrupt you, because we, over the Bush administration and others, have relied upon the Nigerian forces in years back to be one of the strongest. So you are now thinking they are weakened?

Mr. GARTENSTEIN-ROSS. Well, with the specific militaries going after Boko Haram, I think that they are the most challenged. One of the problems that the Nigerian military has today is corruption and lack of morale have made it a worse force than it was a decade ago.

Ms. JACKSON LEE. So President Buhari has not been able to keep his word that they would be extinguished by December 2015?

Mr. GARTENSTEIN-ROSS. Oh, unequivocally not. I mean, extinguished is a very particular thing. No one would say they are extinguished.

Ms. JACKSON LEE. It is a deafening word. As I look at the map, I see that the countries of Niger, Benin, and Cameroon, as I understand it Boko Haram has seeped over into those areas. Is that not accurate?

Mr. GARTENSTEIN-ROSS. Yes.

Ms. JACKSON LEE. They have crossed over the border and maybe even to Chad?

Mr. GARTENSTEIN-ROSS. Yes.

Ms. JACKSON LEE. Because the coloration ends around Nigeria but they go in and out, do they not?

Mr. GARTENSTEIN-ROSS. Yes, it has carried out major attacks in Niger, Chad and Cameroon.

Ms. JACKSON LEE. Right. And so the forces that you were speaking of is some of these troops from the surrounding countries. Which would you be to see as seem to be the strongest?

Mr. GARTENSTEIN-ROSS. I would defer on that in that I would want to actually try to do an assessment. But just what I can say is that Nigerians are, their military is particularly challenged right now, and looking at kind of the battlefield others have been better. Perhaps one of my colleagues can speak to military capabilities, comparison of the four.

Ms. FRIEND. Congresswoman, if I may. You are absolutely right that the Nigerians used to be one of the best militaries in Africa. There was at least a decade of underinvestment, however, in part because of concerns about a military coup. And so the forces that met with Boko Haram were incredibly under equipped, ill-trained, their morale was very low.

What Buhari has done since coming into office which he hasn't even been in for a year yet and these things take a long time, which is part of what I think the U.S. needs to remember is a little bit of patience to let them recapitalize. But I think one of the things he has done that has been particularly inspiring for the foot soldiers is clean out some of the brass at the top, say we are going to have a different kind of command climate. He is himself a retired major general in the army.

So he has had a real focus on trying to improve morale, again personnel payment, and then equipment from sort of all sources he can get to build the forces back up again. But it is going to take time. So right now it is not the Nigerian military that you might remember from years past.

Ms. JACKSON LEE. Let me conclude, and bells are ringing on me. Let me conclude, bells are ringing, by saying, and I am glad you gave me that opening. I do want to acknowledge the strength of President Buhari's words and I would associate with his commitment.

So I would like to leave the record—and I want to thank the chairman. I would like to leave the record with indicating that the map coloration, the bleeding of Boko Haram is outside the borders of Nigeria and so they are terrorizing many of the surrounding countries. I have offered that I believe this is an African Union issue, a United Nations issue. Comments were made about Africa. Most of the world is destabilized. The Mideast, it gives me pause to find outside of Israel one stabilized country in the Mideast, Jordan, let me not, and there may be one or two others, but we are facing an unusual terroristic siege, if you will.

So I guess I would like to leave on the record that Boko Haram attention needs to be enhanced. It took great pride in associating itself with ISIL. It is as dangerous or worse as my colleague has said. And I do believe that we need to put pressure on Europe.

We have the Africa Command, we have the Leahy rule, and we need to find some flexibility where we can work with those resources and those military resources in a way that says that we mean business in the terms of the security of those areas, because they will do nothing but grow and continue their siege of horrific violence. And I thank you all. With that, Mr. Chairman, I yield back.

Mr. POE. I thank the gentlelady, and I thank both Ms. Jackson Lee and Ms. Wilson for their being here today and also their strong interest in this very tragic situation.

Without objection, the chair will recognize Mr. Keating for an additional question.

Mr. KEATING. Thank you, Mr. Chair. Just one final question that we had regarding your testimony and just as an overview. Over 200 girls missing, a mystery, no trace of them alive or killed, no trace whatsoever. That makes me question the extent and capabilities of Nigeria's domestic intelligence on the ground and U.S. intelligence on the ground. Can you comment on our current capabilities and what some of our needs might be and both Nigeria's needs in terms of intelligence and our own?

Ms. FRIEND. I can take a try at it. So immediately after the Chibok kidnapping, the Department of Defense announced that it was providing ISR supports which of course is overhead surveillance, and now there is also ISR support coming out of Cameroon as well. Again that is overhead surveillance.

On the ground penetration into northern Nigeria by almost anyone who is not a resident there or part of a military contingent is very thin. Lots of NGOs can't get in. And so my sense has always been that our on the ground intelligence has been really reliant on the Nigerians and on other sources, and that most of what we do and most of our support to Nigeria has been through ISR which is a huge technical capability that they of course do not have.

In terms of intelligence sharing, again what we share has to be capitalized on by the Nigerians.

Mr. KEATING. Thank you. And I would just say that given Boko Haram's allegiance to ISIL, it is even more important, I think, the U.S. to have more active intelligence on the ground. Thank you very much.

Mr. POE. I thank the gentleman. I thank all y'all for being here today. All y'all is plural to you all in case you are wondering. But thank you for the work that you do, and there may be other questions that members of the committee have for you more specific and they will file those questions within the next 5 days and we would appreciate your prompt response to those questions. And thank you for your expertise in this very tragic area. Thank you very much. The committee is adjourned.

[Whereupon, at 3:19 p.m., the subcommittee adjourned.]

A P P E N D I X

MATERIAL SUBMITTED FOR THE RECORD

SUBCOMMITTEE HEARING NOTICE
COMMITTEE ON FOREIGN AFFAIRS
U.S. HOUSE OF REPRESENTATIVES
WASHINGTON, DC 20515-6128

Subcommittee on Terrorism, Nonproliferation, and Trade
Ted Poe (R-TX), Chairman

TO: MEMBERS OF THE COMMITTEE ON FOREIGN AFFAIRS

You are respectfully requested to attend an OPEN hearing of the Committee on Foreign Affairs. to be held by the Subcommittee on Terrorism, Nonproliferation, and Trade in Room 2200 of the Rayburn House Office Building (and available live on the Committee website at http://www.ForeignAffairs.house.gov):

DATE: Wednesday, February 24, 2016

TIME: 2:00 p.m.

SUBJECT: Boko Haram: The Islamist Insurgency in West Africa

WITNESSES: Ms. Jennifer G. Cooke
                   Director
                   Africa Program
                   Center for International and Strategic Studies

                   Mr. Jacob Zenn
                   Fellow
                   African and Eurasian Affairs
                   The Jamestown Foundation

                   Daveed Gartenstein-Ross, Ph.D.
                   Senior Fellow
                   Foundation for Defense of Democracies

                   Ms. Alice Hunt Friend
                   Adjunct Senior Fellow
                   Center for New American Security

By Direction of the Chairman

COMMITTEE ON FOREIGN AFFAIRS

MINUTES OF SUBCOMMITTEE ON _____ *Terrorism Nonproliferation and Trade* _____ HEARING

Day __*Wednesday*__ Date __*February 24, 2016*__ Room _____ *2200* _____

Starting Time __*2:01 p.m.*__ Ending Time __*3:19 p.m.*__

Recesses |____| (____to ____) (____to ____) (____to ____) (____to ____) (____to ____) (____to ____)

Presiding Member(s)

Chairman Ted Poe, Rep. Scott Perry (2:52 p.m. - 3:00 p.m.)

Check all of the following that apply:

Open Session ☑
Executive (closed) Session ☐
Televised ☑

Electronically Recorded (taped) ☑
Stenographic Record ☑

TITLE OF HEARING:

"Boko Haram: The Islamist Insurgency in West Africa"

SUBCOMMITTEE MEMBERS PRESENT:

Reps. Poe, Perry, Zeldin, Keating, Higgins

NON-SUBCOMMITTEE MEMBERS PRESENT: *(Mark with an * if they are not members of full committee.)*

Reps. Jackson Lee, Wilson (FL)**

HEARING WITNESSES: Same as meeting notice attached? Yes ☐ No ☑
(If "no", please list below and include title, agency, department, or organization.)

Ms. Jennifer G. Cooke - Director, Africa Program, Center for International & strategic Studies
Dr. Daveed Gartenstein-Ross - Senior Fellowm Foundation for Defense of Democracies
Ms. Alice Hunt Friend - Adjunct Senior Fellow, Center for New American Security

STATEMENTS FOR THE RECORD: *(List any statements submitted for the record.)*

SFR: submitted by Mr. Jacob Zenn - African and Eurasian Affairs Fellow, The Jamestown Foundation (He was asked to be a witness, but was unable to attend the hearing due to unforeseen travel difficulties.)

TIME SCHEDULED TO RECONVENE _____
or
TIME ADJOURNED __*3:19 p.m.*__

The JAMESTOWN
F O U N D A T I O N

"Boko Haram and the Islamist Insurgency in West Africa"
Testimony before the U.S. House of Representatives,
Committee on Foreign Affairs,
Terrorism, Non-Proliferation, and Trade Subcommittee
February 24, 2016

Members of Congress, Ladies and Gentlemen:

My name is Jacob Zenn. I am a Fellow of African and Eurasian Affairs at The Jamestown Foundation. The views I express in this testimony are my own.

Thank you for inviting me to testify before you today on the topic of "Boko Haram and the Islamist Insurgency in West Africa."

In this testimony, I will answer the following questions:

1. **Is Boko Haram ("Islamic State in West Africa Province") part of Islamic State (also known as ISIS, ISIL, Al-Baghdadi's Organization or Daesh) and, if so: [PAGES 2-3]**

   a. **what does the instability in Libya and Islamic State's presence in Libya mean for Boko Haram; and [PAGES 3-5]**

   b. **how does Islamic State feature in the structure of Boko Haram? [PAGES 5-6]**

2. **Does Islamic State, particularly its "Provinces" in Libya, have a *transformative* impact on Boko Haram activities in the Lake Chad sub-region (Nigeria, Niger, Chad and Cameroon)? [PAGES 7-9]**

3. **Does Al-Qaeda or its affiliate Al-Qaeda in the Islamic Maghreb (AQIM) still influence Boko Haram and, if not: [PAGES 9-11]**

   a. **what is the probability that AQIM and Boko Haram will form an alliance in the future? [PAGES 12-13]**

4. **How can US Counterterrorism strategy more effectively counter the Islamist insurgencies in West Africa and Boko Haram in particular? [PAGES 13-15]**

1. Is Boko Haram ("Islamic State in West Africa Province") part of Islamic State (also known as ISIS, ISIL, Al-Baghdadi's Organization or Daesh)?

Based on primary source materials, the answer is irrefutably "yes."

On March 7, 2015, Boko Haram leader and spokesman Abubakr Shekau pledged *baya*, or allegiance, to Islamic State leader, or "Caliph", Abubakr Al-Baghdadi.[1]

This pledge followed a "courtship process" between Boko Haram and Islamic State that began shortly after Boko Haram kidnapped more than 250 schoolgirls in Chibok in April 2014 and lasted until March 7, 2015.[2]

On March 8, 2015, Islamic State recognized Shekau's pledge in its Al-Bayan News Bulletin. On March 12, 2015, the spokesman for Islamic State leader Abubakr Al-Baghdadi, Abu Muhammed Al-Adnani, also explicitly accepted Shekau's pledge.[3] On Page 14 in Islamic State's online magazine, *Dabiq 8*, in July 2015, Islamic State also recognized the pledge.[4] In *Dabiq 9*, Islamic State even suggested that a nuclear weapon could be taken from Pakistan overland to Libya and then from Libya to Nigeria and sent from the shores of Nigeria to America along sea routes used by drug smugglers. This is perhaps not so concerning that such a scenario is likely to happen but that Islamic State is saying that if it *could* get chemical, biological or nuclear weapons it would have no problem using them (it has used chemical weapons in Iraq and Syria already).

In two editions of Islamic State's magazine *Dabiq* from before the pledge, Islamic State had already praised the Chibok kidnapping by the "Nigerian mujahidin" and acknowledged that a pledge was made to Islamic State by Boko Haram but that there was not the necessary unity to formally recognize it (perhaps the Ansaru faction had not yet agreed to join the pledge with Boko Haram to Islamic State). Islamic State supporters throughout 2014 on social media were constantly asking when the Boko Haram pledge to the "Caliphate" would happen. Thus, once Shekau made his pledge to Al-Baghdadi, Islamic State media teams in Syria, Iraq, Yemen and Algeria showed "parades" of fighters to celebrate Boko Haram joining Islamic State. This further shored up Shekau's support among factions that had been indifferent about the pledge by proving that Islamic State enthusiastically recognized the pledge. At that time, the video series was the most widespread messaging campaign that Islamic State had carried out.

The following "Provinces" released such videos celebrating Boko Haram's pledge:

- Al-Barakah[5]
- Homs[6]
- Halab (Aleppo)[7]
- Al-Jazirah[8]
- Al-Furat[9]
- Al-Janub[10]
- Al-Raqqa (twice)[11]
- Al-Khayr[12]
- Diglah[13]

Since Shekau's pledge to Al-Baghdadi in March 2015, 100% of Boko Haram's approximately 30 media releases have been through Islamic State media channels. These releases focused on the idea of Boko Haram holding territory, which is key to Islamic State's legitimacy as a "Caliphate." Other videos have included a group of Boko Haram militants putting their hands together and pledging *baya* to Al-Baghdadi and a Boko Haram militant encouraging "Somali mujahidin (Al-Shabab)" to defect from Al-Qaeda and join Islamic State.

Islamic State shows Shekau's pledge in Arabic with English and French subtitles at a cafe in Libya (2015)

a. What importance does the instability in Libya and Islamic State's presence in Libya mean for Boko Haram?

Individual wealthy Nigerians have joined Islamic State in Syria, but not necessarily as members of Boko Haram and rather in an independent capacity. There are, however, increasing reports from Nigerian security forces of arrests of Nigerians "migrating" to Libya (instead of Syria) to join Islamic State as well as tweets from Islamic State members in Libya saying "Shekau's followers" arrived in Libya. Libyan and Algerian researchers of Boko Haram also suggest Boko Haram members are fighting with Islamic State in the country. Moreover, a commander of Islamic State in Benghazi was named Walid Al-Bernawi, suggesting he (or his descendants) were from Borno State, Nigeria or its environs.

Based on recent arrests of radicalized university students in Nigeria who expressed interest in joining Islamic State, there is a concern that Islamic State will encourage "lone-wolf" style attacks in sub-Saharan Africa. This would be a divergence from the "collective" attacks that have characterized violent activity in the region in the past. In the case of Nigeria, "lone-wolf" attacks would be an Islamic State-induced "tactical innovation" in the likes of those that Al-Qaeda brought to the country in 2011, when Nigeria suffered its first ever suicide bombings in 2011, such as the UN Headquarters attack in Abuja. At that time leading experts from Nigeria and abroad had thought such Al-Qaeda-style attacks would be impossible in the country; now Nigeria may be bracing for "Islamic State-style" attacks in the future, whether "lone-wolf" atacks or in the model of the Paris or (failed) Jakarta "urban invasion" attacks in November 2015 and January 2016, respectively.

My interviews of officials in Niger also conclude that Boko Haram easily travels from Nigeria to Libya through migration routes via Niger or Chad, which are the only two countries separating Libya from Nigeria. In addition, Arabic-speaking Libya-based mercenaries who were formerly in Muammar Qaddafi's army and are capable of driving and repairing tanks have also used Chad and Sudan as a transit point. The role of Sudanese (and Cameroonian) Boko Haram members in Boko Haram's Islamic State-trained media team in advance of and following Shekau's pledge suggests that Sudan was also a "bridge" between Boko Haram and Islamic State. Its universities were also a recruitment hub for the Al-Qaeda-borne faction of Boko Haram known as Ansaru, which like Boko Haram, was designated a terrorist organization by the U.S in 2013. The Chadian tank-drivers, in particular, supported Boko Haram during its "occupation" of large swathes of northeastern Nigeria in 2014, when Shekau four times declared an "Islamic State" in Nigeria.

My research also concludes that a Libya/Tunisia-based Islamic State-endorsed media organization called Africa Media segued the connections between Boko Haram and Islamic State leadership to enable Shekau's pledge. A former associate with Ansaru told me Boko Haram now reports to Libya in the Islamic State hierarchy. This is consistent with the role of Islamic State in Libya also coordinating relations with pro-Islamic State factions in Somalia. Former Ansaru members, who were initially intended to be united with Boko Haram but did not do so due to ideological differences with Shekau, have nonetheless since accepted Shekau role as leader. These Ansaru members played a key role connecting Shekau to other Islamic State factions in North Africa that, like Ansaru, defected from AQIM to Islamic State (this can be determined through rigorous analysis of Boko Haram's strategic communications and tactics, techniques and procedures, or TTPs, since mid-2014 as well as other data, such as incidents of former Ansaru militants turning up in Boko Haram's ranks, joint claims, and review of trends of allegiances of allied former Al-Qaeda militants in northwestern Africa). In fact, Shekau's appearance in only two audios and no videos since making the pledge to Al-Baghdadi is consistent with Islamic State's template for leaders, or *walis*, of "Provinces" to not have a public persona (that could upstage Al-Baghdadi) and corroborates Islamic State's impact on Boko Haram's new strategic communication operation since the pledge.

Nonetheless, the fact that the pledge to Islamic State finally put Shekau on the backstage, which Ansaru may have wanted all along, may be part of an Al-Qaeda plot espoused by Abu Iyyad Al-Tunisi to "moderate" Boko Haram by infiltrating it, similar to what Al-Qaeda in the Arabian Peninsula (AQAP) seems to be doing to Islamic State in Yemen.

Finally, it is important to recall that prior to Shekau's allegiance to Islamic State, there was little evidence of Boko Haram activities in Libya. The farthest region Boko Haram, or Ansaru, fighters were seen was in Mali and northern Niger. The Libyan connection evolved with trust built after Shekau's allegiance to Al-Baghdadi. Libya is in a state of civil, tribal, and factional war and offers a ground to train the next generation of fighters for Boko Haram, or unaffiliated Nigerian militants, such as Abu Dujana Al-Nigeri, who Islamic State in Libya eulogized in a statement on February 15, 2016. This is similar to the situation of Boko Haram after 2009, when commanders went abroad and trained with AQIM and Al-Shabab and brought new tactics back to Nigeria. Now a new crop of fighters can be trained in more sophisticated tactics, such as rocket production and strategic communication, in Libya. Although at present Islamic State in Libya is focused on consolidation of control in Sirte and nearby oil installations, it will continue to invest in sub-Saharan African co-Provinces.

In late 2015, in addition to Boko Haram (and Ansaru) members "migrating" to Libya, there were also Senegalese funding networks of Boko Haram in Niger. This coincided with reports of a Senegalese "colony" in Sirte, Libya, which is under Islamic State control are arrests of a Boko Haram cell in Sengal. The Senegalese ties to Boko Haram may therefore be maturing.

Senegalese "colony" in Sirte, Libya under "Islamic State in West Africa Province" (2016)[14]

b. How does Islamic State feature in the structure of Boko Haram?

It is important to understand that Islamic State (like Al-Qaeda before it) provides a "super-structure" for Boko Haram. This means Islamic State provides strategic-level support, such as media and narrative development and attack targeting and operational recommendations, as well as funding and recruitment and training in Libya. Al-Qaeda via AQIM was, however, more tactical in its support to Boko Haram's networks in Nigeria. AQIM's project, Ansaru, carried out kidnappings of foreigners in Nigeria in coordination with AQIM, while AQIM trainees orchestrated major attacks, including the first suicide bombings that targeted churches in the Middle Belt region and at the UN Headquarters in Abuja in August 2011.

The Mapping below shows Islamic State as part of the "super-structure" of Boko Haram with a yellow perforated line signifying how Islamic State has merged fluidly with Boko Haram, especially via their respective media wings. The Mapping was 'validated' in a two-day meeting with leading northern Nigerian politicians, religious scholars, barristers, and individuals, who knew Boko Haram founder Muhammed Yusuf and Shekau and Ansaru commanders personally, as well as security officers who worked on frontlines against Boko Haram. It was also based on field research in Nigeria, Niger, Chad and Cameroon in 2015.

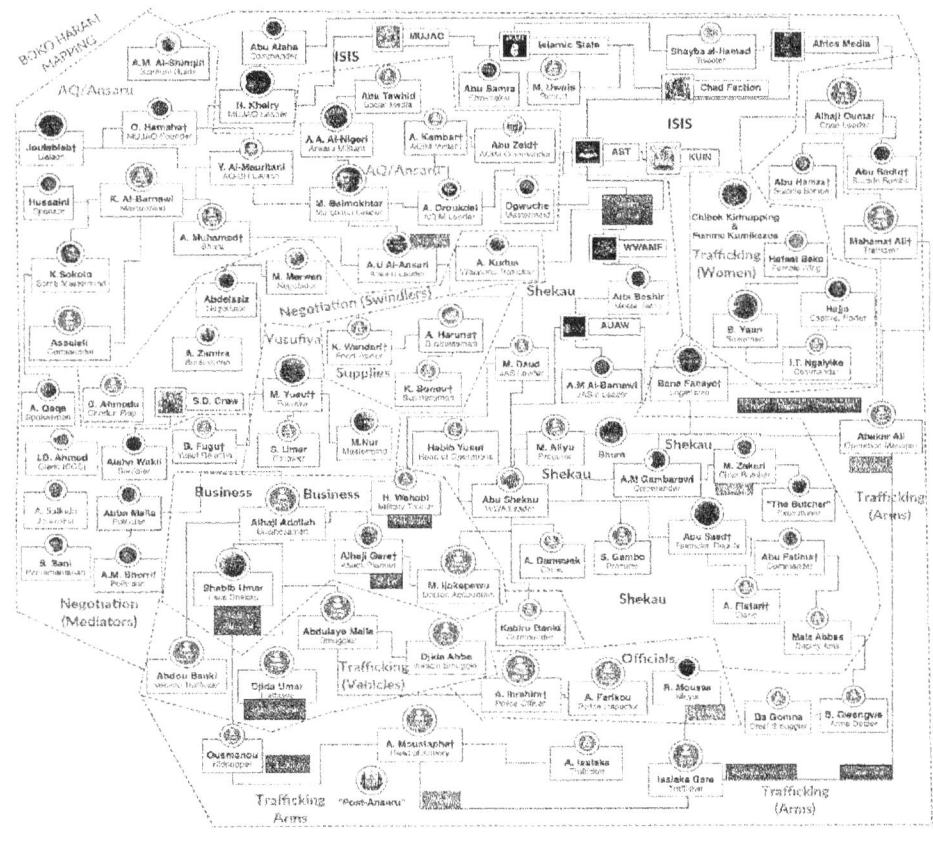

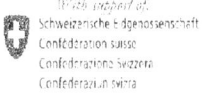

With support of:
Schweizerische Eidgenossenschaft
Confédération suisse
Confederazione Svizzera
Confederaziun svizra

Federal Department of Foreign Affairs FDFA

Draft of December 2015.
For more details contact the author.

The JAMESTOWN
F O U N D A T I O N

2. Does Islamic State, particularly its "Provinces" in Libya, have a transformative impact on Boko Haram activities in the Lake Chad sub-region (Nigeria, Niger, Chad and Cameroon)?

Now that it is established that Islamic State and Boko Haram are merged on a leadership and organizational level, one of the key questions is whether Islamic State has, or will have, a *transformative* impact on Boko Haram?

Thus far, from Shekau's reduced role in Boko Haram videos, to the Al-Urhwa Al-Wutqha twitter account that Islamic State set up with Boko Haram in advance of Shekau's pledge to Al-Baghdadi, to the Boko Haram videos and statistical "infographics" released through Islamic State channels since March 2015, the **strategic communication** of both groups are fully integrated. Since Islamic State relies so much on strategic communication—especially social media—to propagate its narrative and recruit new militants (as well as doctors and other "service-providers") from around the world to its Caliphate, the fact that Boko Haram has allowed Islamic State to coordinate its strategic communication is a significant development. This is especially the case in the context of Islamic State encouraging foreign fighters, especially Africans, to "migrate" to Libya or Nigeria if they cannot make it to Syria.

There are other indications of Islamic State impact on Boko Haram. This includes the decision of Boko Haram to **hold territory** that included several dozen towns in northeastern Nigeria in 2014. Shekau declared these areas to be part of an "Islamic State" (in Hausa, *dawlat Musulunci*, and Arabic, *dawla Islamiya*) at least four times in 2014. In contrast, before 2014, Boko Haram was mostly engaged in hit-and-run operations or large-scale bombings. Holding territory in the lead-up to Shekau's pledge to Al-Baghdadi not only impressed Islamic State but also indicated that Boko Haram could "serve" Al-Baghdadi's Caliphate and fulfill the crucial requirement that a Caliphate must hold territory (the other two requirements are that Al-Baghdadi is from the Qurayshi Arab tribe and that he has, according to Islamic State, the support of Islamic scholars, or *ulema*).

In addition, Boko Haram made a strategic decision in 2014 to carry out consistent attacks and **expand operationally** in Cameroon, Chad and Niger (previously Boko Haram's attacks in these countries were sporadic, although it had raised millions of dollars and secured weapons traffickers from prison via the kidnapping-for-ransom of more than 20 foreigners in Cameroon in 2013-2014). These attacks on Nigeria's neighbors, in particular, were promoted on the Islamic State-endorsed Africa Media twitter account that operated with Boko Haram's own twitter account called Al-Urhwa Al-Wutqha. Expanding beyond Nigeria and activating cells in neighboring countries that were previously focused on trafficking weapons, arms, and (kidnapped) women also served the "Islamic State in West Africa Province" narrative by showing that the new Province was not limited to the nation-state of Nigeria but rather the entire Provincial region—West Africa—that the Islamic State designated for it. Thus, the new Boko Haram cells in Senegal that reportedly are under Shekau's leadership could be an extension of the trans-national campaign that first reached into Nigeria's borderlands and the Lake Chad sub-region in 2014.

Nonetheless, Boko Haram's attacks in the Lake Chad sub-region can also be attributed to retaliation by Boko Haram on Niger, Chad and Cameroon for their breaking up of Boko Haram cells in their countries in 2014 and entering Nigerian territory as part of the Multi-Natinal Joint Task Force (MNTJF) (although Boko Haram retaliatory threats in statements to these countries seem to have been drafted with Africa Media). Nigeria's neighbors helped force Boko Haram to abandon Shekau's declared "Islamic State", including its "capital" of Gwoza, which Boko Haram renamed "Dar al-Hikma (*House of Wisdom* in Arabic)". Since 2014, Boko Haram has become as active in northern Cameroon as Nigeria. Boko Haram's attacks against Chad in Chad and Chadian troops in Cameroon also seem to have neutralized Chadian forces, which withdrew from Cameroon in 2015. It should also be recognized that in context of Boko Haram's "conquests" in Nigeria, the Nigerian military—in part due to low morale and low resourcing due to misallocated funds, corruption and unaccountability—had collapsed in some areas, leaving large swathes of territory to Boko Haram for the taking.

In terms of promoting attacks, it is notable that since Shekau's pledge Islamic State has claimed only five specific attacks by Boko Haram all of which had a large media impact or targeted enemies that show a regional, or West African, focus, including:

- 4 suicide attacks in N'djamena and Borno (June 2015);
- 3 bombings in Abuja (October 2015);
- Attack "Infographics" against (October and December 2015) (via *Al-Amaq* Agency);
    - Nigerian Army, Chadian Army, Nigerien Army, Cameroon Army
    - Pro-Government Gunmen
    - Pro-Government Parties
    - Shiite Militias
- Attack on a Shia procession in Kano (December 2015); and
- 3 bombings of "militias" in Cameroon (January 2016) (via *Al-Amaq* Agency).

Another often overlooked area of Islamic State influence on Boko Haram, especially given leadership relations between Shekau and Islamic State is the area of **negotiation**. It is unlikely now that militants under Shekau can come to a ceasefire with Nigeria or neighboring governments without Islamic State approval, since any ceasefire would impact Islamic State's overall brand. Such a ceasefire may, at this point, work if it included a Boko Haram demand for an autonomous Islamic State in Borno, which is untenable for Nigeria.

Yet, the issue of negotiations also extends to the Chibok schoolgirls. Circumstantial evidence suggests that Boko Haram militants behind this kidnapping operate under Islamic State's banner. An indication of this comes from the second Chibok video featuring Shekau, which showed a Shekau speech and then displayed about 100 kidnapped girls. For one of the first times Boko Haram used the Islamic State-styled flag in the background. This video also had production details similar to previous Boko Haram-released Maiduguri Air Base and Giwa Barracks attack videos. Based on the types of TTPs in those barracks attacks and in Chibok, they likely involved the former Ansaru or Mali-based cross-border "ambush" teams that also attacked military barracks in Borno State in 2013-2014.

In the first Chibok video featuring Shekau, Shekau also chanted Islaimc State slogans (*dawlat al-Islam qamai, dawlat al-Isam baqiya*) and for the first time referenced the previously exclusively Ansaru narrative of Usman dan Fodio. Moreover, Islamic State recognized the Chibok kidnapping in its magazine *Dabiq* and via the Tunisia/Libya-based media outlet Africa Media. It is also important to consider that the Chibok kidnapping reflects Ansaru TTPs and "post-Ansaru" networks seem to be involved in the female suicide bombings, which do not employ the Chibok girls but began only two months after the Chibok kidnappings and have since involved nearly 200 girl "attackers" in a 20-month period. It appears that the faction behind the Chibok kidnapping (a pro-Islamic State formerly Ansaru-connected one coordinating with Shekau) relates to the one behind female suicide bombings, possibly under oversight of ex-Ansaru commander Khalid Al-Barnawi.

A screenshot of the second video of the Chibok schoolgirls shows an Islamic State-styled flag, which was then new for Boko Haram, and a uniformed militant filming and "interviewing" the girls (May 2014)

3. Does Al-Qaeda or its affiliate AQIM still influence Boko Haram?

o Macro-picture

At first, it is important to understand the activities of Al-Qaeada on a macro-level both globally and in Africa in response to the "rise" of the Islamic State in 2014 and its "expansion" to Africa in 2015. The below discussion provides a re-hashing.

In 2015, Islamic State emerged on the *international scene* (as opposed to the Iraqi-Syrian scene) with the declaration of "Provinces" outside the Middle East, such as in Khorasan (Afghanistan) and West Africa (Boko Haram). Islamic State also secured defections from Al-Qaeda in the Islamic Maghreb (AQIM) factions (but not the leadership), including five ones in Algeria, Movement for Unity and Jihad in West Africa (MUJWA) in Mali, and foot soldiers in Katibat Uqba Ibn Nafi (KUIN) and Ansar Al-Sharia Tunisia (AST), both of which are in Tunisia. In East Africa, factions of Al-Shabab, especially those who lived abroad or are from the Swahili Coast, also switched allegiance to Islamic State, likely with financial inducements from Islamic State. Some Al-Shabab factions, however, seem to regret their defection and note Islamic State abandoned them after Al-Shabab started killing them.

The JAMESTOWN
F O U N D A T I O N

Despite Islamic State's emergence in Africa, in late 2015 Al-Qaeda began to rebound. AQIM launched attacks on hotels in Bamako, Mali and Ouagadougou, Burkina Faso (both formerly outside of AQIM's regular area of operations) and continued ambushes on UN and Malian troops in coordination with allied militants in Ansar Dine and Macina Liberation Front (FLM). Meanwhile, Al-Shabab in late 2015 carried out attacks on Kenya Defense Forces (KDF) and took back territory from AMISOM in Somalia and launched attacks in Kenya.

AQIM and Al-Shabab also ramped up attacks on defectors who pledged to Al-Baghdadi. But rather than "advertise" such attacks, Al-Qaeda stayed silent to avoid the image of "killing other Muslims". This "silence", in particular, is consistent with Al-Qaeda strategy dating to the time of Usama bin Laden and is implemented across Al-Qaeda affiliates and allied militant groups from AQIM and Al-Shabab in Africa, to Taliban to Al-Qaeda in the Arabian Peninsula (AQAP) in Yemen to Jabhat Al-Nusra in Syria. Also consistent across Al-Qaeda affiliates is their ideological rejection and discrediting of Al-Baghdadi's declared Caliphate.

The "strategic continuity" among Al-Qaeda affiliates in countering Islamic State is likely facilitated by a higher level of communication between affiliates than is regularly believed. For example, a letter shared between an Al-Qaeda leader in Tunisia, Abu Iyad Al-Tunisi, to Al-Qaeda leader Ayman Al-Zawahiri (reportedly with Shekau and other Al-Qaeda-aligned leader in "CC") urging Al-Qaeda to infiltrate and subvert Islamic State so as to make it adopt a doctrine more like Al-Qaeda is one example that Al-Qaeda communications and strategizing is ongoing. In fact, Ansaru members *may* have adopted Al-Tunisi's plan in re-joining with Boko Haram under Islamic State's overall leadership.

o   Micro-picture

In Africa, Al-Qaeda has more entrenched roots than Islamic State. Several African Al-Qaeda operatives, including ex-Ansaru commander Khalid Al-Barnawi, gave *baya* to Bin Laden in Sudan in the 1990s. "Proto-Al-Qaeda" was involved in U.S. embassy bombings in the late 1990s in Kenya and Tanzania (and USS Cole off the coast of Yemen). Al-Shabab members had also been based in Sudan when Bin Laden lived there. AQIM commanders, such as Mokhtar Belmokhtar, fought in Afghanistan when Bin Laden and the Taliban formed what became the Al-Qaeda that attacked the U.S. on 9/11. They returned home to set up affiliates in North Africa. As such, despite pressure Islamic State places on Al-Qaeda, Al-Qaeda is likely to count on its roots in Africa to persist in spite of this new challenge.

Al-Qaeda also has a "localization" strategy that is not unique to its operations in Africa, but has become pronounced in West Africa. According to this strategy, Al-Qaeda embeds itself in—or infiltrates—local groups, populations and potentially NGOs or municipal or tribal structures, which Al-Qaeda calls the "third circle" (Al-Qaeda Central is "first circle" and known affiliates are "second circle"). "Third circle" groups do not use the name "Al-Qaeda" or make known relations to Al-Qaeda, even while they further Al-Qaeda objectives. They, in essence, operate behind enemy lines whether in the West or hostile locations in Africa.

One example of a group operating in between in the "second circle" and "third circle" is the FLM, which operates in Southern Mali and is comprised of ethnic Fulanis and caters to Fulani narratives of the Caliphate. The use of the word "Macina"—an historical Fulani emirate—and "Liberation"—to hide its Jihadist ambitions—is an example of this Al-Qaeda strategy. In actuality, FLM carries out attacks in coordination with AQIM; notably, two militants in the hotel attack at the Radisson Blu in Bamako carried the *nisba* Al-Fulani and so did one militant in the attack on Splendid Hotel in Ouagadougou (both AQIM and the FLM as well as Ansar Dine and Al-Mourabitun also took part in the claim of the attack on the Radisson Blu). Al-Qaeda's exploitation and "managed separation" of sub-affiliates to form "second/third circle" groups, such as MUJAO in Mali and Ansaru in Nigeria, differs from Islamic State's *modus operandi*. Whereas Al-Qaeda is more about the "core" serving the "local" groups as part of a broader decentralization and expansion strategy, Islamic State is more about the "local" groups, or Provinces, serving the "core" in Al-Raqqa or Mosul (or Sirte, Libya), so as to promote the narrative and goals of Al-Baghdadi's Caliphate.

Given ongoing animosity between Al-Qaeda and Islamic State and Shekau's pledge to Al-Baghdadi, it is not likely, however, that AQIM is substantially influencing Boko Haram at this moment. Nonetheless, AQIM is likely strategizing about a way to re-enter the Nigerian scene (as well as countries like Central African Republic) and win not only new recruits but defectors from Boko Haram under Islamic State back to Al-Qaeda.

The AQIM Anadalus Media-claimed kidnapping of German engineer Fritz Raupach in Kano in 2012 by a cell led by two Mauritanian militants was among the first explicit signs AQIM was operating in Nigeria.

a. What is the probability that AQIM and Boko Haram will form an alliance in the future?

One way Al-Qaeda is responding to Islamic State and making a "comeback" since late 2015 is by an 'Open Door Policy' for defectors to Islamic State (and other disaffected Islamic State militants) to rejoin Al-Qaeda. If Islamic State suffers setbacks in Syria and the "Caliphate" is unraveled, or if Islamic State militants are alienated due to its brutality especially against Muslims, some Islamic State militants may return to Al-Qaeda, including those in Boko Haram (and especially former Ansaru members).

Given Al-Qaeda's increasing operations in West Africa, one question is whether it can make a comeback in Nigeria, where from 2011-2013 it oversaw the creation of Ansaru as a faction ideologically opposed to Boko Haram but operationally more sophisticated that targeted mostly foreigners. Ansaru, however, became defunct after the French-led military intervention in Mali in 2013, with some members returning to Boko Haram and later becoming loyal to or at least tolerating Shekau and pledging *baya* to Al-Baghdadi. These Ansaru members who are now working with Boko Haram may still have divided loyalties and may view AQIM as a better umbrella than Islamic State but for survival and sustenance are now tolerating—or seeking to moderate—Shekau's leadership.

Notably, Boko Haram even after joining Islamic State is one of the only Islamic State Provinces to avoid polemical exchanges against Al-Qaeda, suggesting it may still have a "soft spot" for its former patrons. Ex-Ansaru members also seem to have been at the forefront of Boko Haram media since Boko Haram opened the twitter account that led to Shekau's pledge in early 2015, so they may now be a "gatekeeper" preventing such anti-Al-Qaeda messaging. This may even be one reason why since late 2015 Boko Haram media releases have come to a seeming halt to an extent that has never been seen before in Boko Haram messaging. In addition, it is important to recognize that pro-Islamic State Africa Media, which brought Boko Haram into the Islamic State media fold via the twitter account, started out 'above the fray' when it came to the Islamic State-Al-Qaeda rivalry. Africa Media may have left a "tolerant" legacy on the former Ansaru members and Shekau factions that form "Islamic State in West Africa Province" today with regards to opposing Al-Qaeda.

Working against an AQIM re-emergence in Nigeria, however, is that there is little appetite in Nigeria for further Jihadism after the devastation Boko Haram has brought to the region. Thus, the best hope for Al-Qaeda may be that Boko Haram's failure to carry out major attacks in Nigeria after Shekau's pledge and its continued killing of Muslim civilians will lead *already existing militants* to defect to Al-Qaeda. If AQIM can provide a lifeline to them, they may rejoin Al-Qaeda (**thus de-radicalisation and re-integration programs and "opt-outs" for militants are crucial now in Nigeria**). There are likely still factions within Boko Haram, such as ex-Ansaru members, that maintain their contacts to AQIM, which will be crucial in reviving Boko Haram-AQIM relations.

Finally, Boko Haram may still need some support from AQIM-affiliated groups in the Sahel to maintain the current nexus via the Sahel to Islamic State in Libya. Without at least a tacit peace with AQIM in Mali, such communications to Libya will be difficult.

"Visual signatures" from videos on Boko Haram's Islamic State-coordinated twitter account in early 2015, including messaging that civilians could "repent", was suggestive of Ansaru influence.

4. How can US Counterterrorism strategy more effectively counter the Islamist insurgencies in West Africa and Boko Haram in particular?

The following recommendations should be considered:

1. Boko Haram's attacks are not only disproportionate but also unrelated to its supposed grievances. What explains the violence that makes Boko Haram "the deadliest terrorist group" is 1) Al-Qaeda's acceleration of the movement beyond local capabilities and concerns in the 2010-2012 period and later Ansaru's re-integration into Boko Haram and 2) Shekau's role in motivating fighters by drawing on "persecution theory" and exploiting their grievances with the ideology of Global Jihadism. The insurgency is driven by an ideology intertwined with a constellation of local and international perceived grievances, which is why a medical student with a bright future traveled all the way from Nigeria to Libya only to kill himself as a "martyr" because of the belief he is fighting Jihad and sacrificing his life for it.

From a religious perspective, Nigerians note the importance for **counter-narratives that can be encompassed within a Countering Violent Extremism (CVE) programme.** For example, one Nigerian says that, "hope lies in scripture and the tradition of the prophet of Islam, who was balanced in a way that these Mujahidin don't see. For instance you won't find Jihadists citing a *hadith* that translates roughly thus, 'love life like you will never die, love the afterlife like you will die any moment.'" Another Nigerian who knew Muhammed Yusuf follows a *salafi* interpretation that he says compels him to *serve the state. Salafi* and other religious clerics and student leaders with these views need to have their voices amplified and security forces to provide protection for them because they are among the first targets for Boko Haram to assassinate. The Nigerian government can also engage more with Muslim communities and northern intellectuals, elites and traditional rulers to discuss issues, such as the role of *sharia* in the region, and ways to undermine Boko Haram recruitment.

2. The Multi-National Joint Task Force (MNTJF) never really gained its footing. It is now based in Chad, but Chad is seemingly reducing its role in crossing borders to counter Boko Haram in response to Boko Haram-inflicted casualties on its forces. There are also linguistic differences between Nigeria and its French-speaking neighbors. While MNTJF is ideal conceptually, what may be effective is **a series of overlapping sub-regional institutions and agreements designed to combat Boko Haram** as opposed to one over-arching MNTJF, or at least combination of both. For example, Nigeria and Cameroon independently could set parameters for cross-border counter-Boko Haram operations, while the neighbors could set their own three-way policy for countering Boko Haram on islands in Lake Chad.

3. Islamic State in Libya is now actively serving as a "foreign fighter" junction point for Africans in the same way Syria did for Europeans and Central and Southeast Asians in previous years. Boko Haram's alliance with Islamic State and apparent merger also with Senegalese Jihadists in Libya adds a greater **imperative for the U.S. to engage allies in both the Middle East and the West who have resources and commitment to develop a short- and long-term political and military strategy to prevent Libya from becoming the "new Syria" for Islamic State and to share intelligence with Nigeria about "foreign fighters" in Libya**, especially if the coalition "wins" against Islamic State in Syria.

4. The Civilian Joint Task Force (JTF) has performed well and is among the top attack targets of Boko Haram because of its ability to detect Boko Haram cells both in cities like Maiduguri and in villages. At the same time, it is largely unregulated in the villages and could become its own form of enforcement body during this conflict and a "monster" especially after peace is restored. Thus, it is important **Civilian JTF receives training and improves organizational coordination** and sustainability both in the short-term and long-term.

5. Although strictly regulating borders would deprive the people of the Lake Chad region of their "traditional" business and livelihoods, this has already been largely disrupted as a result of Boko Haram. Until the borders are secured so as to prevent an unlimited lifeline of supplies from re-enforcing Boko Haram, it will be difficult to finally "finish-off" the militants. Thus, **enhanced border security in the Lake Chad region and targeting, in particular, of traffickers of arms to Boko Haram is essential** (see Mapping on Page 6).

6. At the heart of Boko Haram's new strategy is targeting Internally Displaced People (IDP) and asymmetric attacks by female suicide bombers to prevent a return to "normalcy" in northeastern Nigeria and keep the people distrusting of the government's ability to provide security. **Timetables can be set up to rebuild towns, roads, schools and infra-structure** so as to more permanently clear Boko Haram from the inter-town routes it now seeks to control and allow people to return home safely and with confidence in their government.

7. The U.S. can **provide military support to Nigeria and neighbors, especially in the form of reconnaissance and counter-Improvised Explosives Device (IED) training**, but it is neither needed nor desirable to engage Boko Haram directly at this time. Rather, the U.S. would be well-off to support national armed forces with a relatively light U.S. footprint.

8. At one conference I attended in Israel, current geopolitical and Violent Non-State Actor (VNSA) trends were described as like a "three-dimensional chess match under water in outer space". In other words, today's conflicts are mired in overlapping alliances, issues and interests and side-order effects (the unintended consequences of the intervention in Libya, for example, had a huge impact on security in Mali and northeastern Nigeria). The U.S. needs to think beyond elections and "quick wins" and instead **think strategically and multi-dimensionally about how to manage adversarial geopolitical and VNSA trends.**

9. The U.S. would be well-off to **cultivate a new generation of scholars and interested professionals in African languages, culture and history** (similar to the U.S. Department of State Critical Language Scholars program, which I participated in for Advanced Indonesian Language in 2011, but with a focus on Africa). Africa will be a center of violent conflict, especially with Islamic State and Al-Qaeda targeting the continent, but it also is a center of innovation and creativity, and U.S. should engage the continent for both reasons.

10. It is important also to **acknowledge recent successes in Nigeria's counter-insurgency strategy** and duplicate and amplify them. These include:

- Targeting Boko Haram logistics routes.
- Eliminating Sambisa Forest and other safe havens.
- Regional / international outreach from the country's leadership but self-dependency.
- Military appointments from insurgent region, who speak Kanuri and local languages.
- Military-familiar leader (who came to power via elections).
- Sustained anti-corruption and accountability focus.
- An IDP plan that despite difficulties has not led to mass extra-regional migration.
- The maintenance and development of the Civilian JTF, despite risks involved.
- Continued efforts with the CVE 'soft approach' despite administrative shake-ups.

Biography: Jacob Zenn is a component leader under EU Technical Assistance to Nigeria's Evolving Security Challenges (EUTANS), and has carried out projects throughout Africa. He is also a Fellow on African and Eurasian Affairs at The Jamestown Foundation. Zenn authored 250-plus reports on Nigeria, Central Asia and Southeast Asia and speaks frequently in academic and popular press and to governments and security personnel. In 2012, he published "Northern Nigeria: The Prize in Al-Qaeda's Africa Strategy."

Zenn consults for clients who need to understand micro-details about leadership, ideology, strategic communication, and operational trends of violent non-state actors (VNSAs)—and particularly those on the "geopolitical periphery" of the Middle East—as well as macro-trends about how VNSAs are evolving in geographical, socio-cultural and historical context.

Zenn holds a J.D. from Georgetown University Law Center, where he was a Global Law Scholar, and a Graduate Certificate in Chinese and American Affairs from Johns Hopkins SAIS-Nanjing University School of Advanced International Studies in China, where courses were taught in Mandarin. Zenn conducts research in more than 10 languages.

Notes (Primary Sources):

1 http://jihadology.net/2015/03/07/al-urwah-al-wuthqa-foundation-presents-a-new-audio-message-from-jamaat-ahl-al-sunnah-li-l-dawah-wa-l-jihad-boko-%E1%B8%A5aram-abu-bakr-shekau-bayah-jama/

2 https://www.ctc.usma.edu/posts/wilayat-west-africa-reboots-for-the-caliphate

3 See 5:20 (http://jihadology.net/2015/03/12/al-furqan-media-presents-a-new-audio-message-from-the-islamic-states-shaykh-abu-mu%E1%B8%A5ammad-al-adnani-al-shami-so-they-kill-and-are-killed/)

4 https://azelin.files.wordpress.com/2015/03/the-islamic-state-e2809cdc481biq-magazine-3e280b3.pdf

5 http://jihadology.net/2015/03/16/new-video-message-from-the-islamic-state-pleasure-of-the-muslims-with-the-bayah-of-their-brothers-in-nigeria-wilayat-al-barakah/

6 http://jihadology.net/2015/03/31/new-video-message-from-the-islamic-state-joy-of-the-mujahidin-of-the-caliphate-state-with-the-bayah-of-their-brothers-in-wilayat-gharb-ifriqiyyah-wilayat-%E1%B8%A5om%E1%B9%A3/

7 http://jihadology.net/2015/03/20/new-video-message-from-the-islamic-state-joy-of-the-monotheists-with-the-bayah-of-the-mujahidin-in-west-africa-wilayat-%E1%B8%A5alab/

8 http://jihadology.net/2015/03/19/new-video-message-from-the-islamic-state-joy-of-the-muslims-with-the-bayah-of-jamaat-ahl-al-sunnah-li-l-dawah-wa-l-jihad-wilayat-al-jazirah/

9 http://jihadology.net/2015/03/16/new-video-message-from-the-islamic-state-the-allegiances-are-coming-and-the-joys-to-the-brothers-in-nigeria-wilayat-al-furat/

10 http://jihadology.net/2015/03/25/new-video-message-from-the-islamic-state-joy-of-the-monotheists-with-the-bayah-of-the-people-of-africa-to-the-caliph-of-the-muslims-wilayat-al-janub/

11 http://jihadology.net/2015/03/15/new-video-message-from-the-islamic-state-advice-to-the-soldiers-of-the-caliphate-in-nigeria-wilayat-al-raqqah/

12 http://jihadology.net/2015/03/12/new-video-message-from-the-islamic-state-joy-of-the-soldiers-of-the-caliphate-with-the-bayah-of-their-brother-in-nigeria-wilayat-al-khayr/

13 http://jihadology.net/2015/03/11/new-video-message-from-the-islamic-state-joy-of-the-monotheists-with-the-bayah-of-the-nigerian-mujahidin-wilayat-diglah/

4 http://www.buzz.sn/news/boko-haram-attirerait-il-autant-de-senegalais-que-la-branche-libyenne-de-lei/34207